THE WRITER'S RETREAT

Dear Traci ~
Thank you for being my inspiration to grow stronger each day! Keep up the good work! Enjoy this lighthearted read. Love ~
Jenny :)

THE WRITER'S RETREAT

JENNY SUE BAKER

NEW DEGREE PRESS

COPYRIGHT © 2022 JENNY SUE BAKER

All rights reserved.

THE WRITER'S RETREAT

ISBN   979-8-88504-523-0   *Paperback*
        979-8-88504-853-8   *Kindle Ebook*
        979-8-88504-529-2   *Ebook*

I'd like to dedicate this book to my husband and children, who supported me through my inaugural attempt at authorship. Your constant belief and encouragement gave me the necessary courage to see this project through until the end. I'd also like to dedicate this book to my friends and family who offered accountability "check ins" along the book-writing journey.

CONTENTS

AUTHOR'S NOTE	11
CHAPTER 1	13
CHAPTER 2	19
CHAPTER 3	27
CHAPTER 4	35
CHAPTER 5	41
CHAPTER 6	49
CHAPTER 7	57
CHAPTER 8	63
CHAPTER 9	69
CHAPTER 10	77
CHAPTER 11	85
CHAPTER 12	93
CHAPTER 13	101
CHAPTER 14	111
CHAPTER 15	123
CHAPTER 16	131
CHAPTER 17	137
CHAPTER 18	145
CHAPTER 19	153
CHAPTER 20	159
CHAPTER 21	169
CHAPTER 22	175
ACKNOWLEDGMENTS	185

"Strange is our situation here on Earth. Each of us comes for a short visit, not knowing why, yet sometimes seeming to divine a purpose. From the standpoint of daily life, however, there is one thing we do know: that man is here for the sake of other men—above all for those upon whose smiles and well-being our own happiness depends."

—ALBERT EINSTEIN

AUTHOR'S NOTE

The pursuit of purpose is all too cliché these days, yet the prevailing, unsettled nag lurks in the minds of many. Being a ponderer of purpose myself, I often question why I'm here, existing in this world. As if I were an ice sculptor, I chip away the excess of each day to unveil the answer, only to be left with the same stirring wonder the next day.

Often I make myself dizzy by walking in circles, trying to decipher which path will lead me to the discovery of purpose or contentment. Adding control of situations around me, rather than loosening the reins and letting life happen, has been my default for too many years. It seems, however, that many of life's best moments are unplanned, unscheduled, and unscripted.

When I signed up to take a writing class last fall, I assumed I'd be learning to write a book when the time felt right, if that time ever came at all. I had to relinquish my expectations of how I thought the class was going to proceed when I found out that, yes, indeed I would be writing a book. My first book!

When I began *The Writer's Retreat*, I didn't have an exact story line mapped out yet because I believed I would find my way once I just got started. I was happily surprised with how it unfolded when I was able to walk the journey of purpose along with my characters.

As I expected, the newness of the writing process was motivating. However, when I encountered obstacles, I was ready to toss in the towel and be done. This book proved to be a delightful challenge—if there is such a thing—in proving I had the tenacity to follow through until the end. It was a test in patience and creativity using insight from real-life scenarios and intertwining them with fictional storytelling.

Travel through my first book with Sarah and Mary as they discover the challenges of love and career as well as the powerful feeling of relinquishing expectations to accept what is. From broken hearts and surrendered careers to serendipitous situations and destined moments—I hope this fictional beach read will resonate with you and your individual pursuit of purpose.

CHAPTER 1

It was a beautiful fall morning in New England, with crisp enough temperatures to see your breath, yet the afternoon sun was waiting to offer the last of summer warmth. Sarah, clutching her steaming coffee cup, waited for the Uber outside her Back Bay apartment building. She anticipated a smooth travel day as the weather forecast looked sunny from Boston to Chicago.

Enjoying the traffic-free route to the airport, Sarah pondered her itinerary and relished in the simplicity of her plan. Just one week and two days ago, Sarah, a columnist for *Simple Travels* magazine, decided that in order to meet her latest deadline, she needed a chunk of uninterrupted days away from her small Boston apartment and the distractions of the city. This deadline was the most important yet of her writing career. She was about to make her dream come true and become a published author of her first book. This Saturday was her deadline. Therefore, renting a small lake cottage in the Midwest would be the perfect way to wrap up her project.

Sarah smiled as she pictured the well-designed vacation rental website where she found her fairytale writing cottage. The detailed descriptions and high-quality photos made the cottage look like the perfect scene for her tranquil writing getaway. Placed on a quaint lake in the Midwest, it boasted two small bedrooms, one bath, and even a screened-in porch where she imagined spending most of her time. She was starting to feel like a "real" author.

Looking back at her travel itinerary, Sarah was pleased with the timing of her day ahead. She thought, *Even with some traffic near O'Hare, I'll be at the cottage and writing by early afternoon.* Smiling once again, she rested her head against the car window and took a relaxing breath while she enjoyed the smooth commute.

Sarah's mood was quickly interrupted when the Uber approached her terminal at Logan Airport. The normal process of dropping her off at the door and driving away was not happening this morning. Cars were lined three rows deep from the sidewalk, horns sounded louder than normal, and people argued with outside ticket agents.

"What the hell is going on here?" Sarah tensely questioned her Uber driver.

"I don't have a clue, lady!" the driver said with a stressed tone. "It's so early, I have hardly finished my coffee, much less listened to the radio." He flipped on the local news station to hear a live broadcast happening right outside of Logan.

"Wait, what did he say?" asked Sarah. "Turn it up, please!"

The driver turned up the volume as the broadcaster mentioned something about flights being canceled or rerouted due to a sudden labor shortage. "What does that even mean, a sudden labor shortage?" the driver asked Sarah. "Maybe they mean the employees went on strike." He'd answered his own question while Sarah tried to get a glimpse of the flurry of activity around her.

Though hesitant, Sarah started to get out of the car.

"You sure you want to stay here, lady? It looks like a complete zoo! I'd be happy to take you back to your place."

Sarah replied, "Thanks for the ride. Hopefully things are better inside the airport. Wish me luck!"

She walked to the curb and stopped to scan the scene. She had traveled in and out of Logan too many times to count but had never witnessed such chaos in every direction. As she took a deep breath and rolled her shoulders back, she thought, *I guess I'm thankful I don't have to deal with checking my bags today.* Then she said, "Well, here goes nothing," walking confidently to the security checkpoint. While waiting in line, she calmly asked those nearby if they knew what was going on. It didn't take long before she realized her idealistic travel day would be nothing like she'd planned.

The phone buzzed in Sarah's pocket. She pulled it out to see a notification from the airline. Her nonstop flight to Chicago had been canceled. *Shit!* With that notification, she heard the volume of cranky travelers raise as they expressed their frustrations toward anyone in line who would listen. Her phone buzzed again with a message from the airline saying she was automatically rebooked on connecting flights through Atlanta and Minneapolis with a final destination in Chicago. The original itinerary had her landing at 11:30 a.m. Now she wouldn't arrive until 4:00 p.m. She shook her head and approached the TSA officer, showing her boarding pass and ID.

Sarah wasn't a stranger to travel disruptions. If anything, she expected them. However, she had never encountered a reason such as a sudden labor shortage. Trying to remain calm, Sarah thought, *Out of my control. It will all be worth it when I'm drinking wine at the cottage tonight.*

Sarah dragged her small carry-on to the gate. Thankful she only needed to pack a few comfortable outfits and some of her running clothes. Though Sarah kept a distance from other travelers, she found it challenging not to absorb some of the angry vibes around her. Fortunately, her frequent flier miles paid off as she was able to board first and was offered a complimentary glass of champagne within minutes of taking her seat.

"Thank you so much!" Sarah said as her flight attendant handed over a glass. "I didn't intend to have a drink this morning, but I'm thinking it might calm my nerves."

"From what we were told, a lot of people have called in sick today. It doesn't affect me at the moment, so I'll just continue on with my day as normal," said the flight attendant, shrugging her shoulders with a hopeful smile. Then she turned to offer champagne to those sitting nearby.

Hearing the frustrated murmurs from the people entering the plane, Sarah took a swig of her champagne before drowning out the noise with her headphones. She rested her head against the headrest, closed her eyes, and let her thoughts drift away with the music.

The rest of Sarah's travel day went as smoothly as could be expected with two connecting flights. With no more delays, she lucked out having arrival and departure gates somewhat close together in Atlanta and Minneapolis. As she waited for her second flight to depart, she found her thoughts going back to her ex-boyfriend, Henry. Though Henry was now engaged to someone else, he and Sarah still kept in touch periodically. She pulled out her phone and texted him a brief message to check-in.

"Hey Henry, how's it going? I hope the wedding plans are coming along. As I've said before, Erin will be a gorgeous bride. I wanted to let you know I am in the home stretch with my book. Final manuscript is due this coming up Saturday! I decided to rent a sweet cottage in the Midwest this week so I can focus on writing without distractions from the city. I'm super excited! My plane is leaving now. Chat soon. Take care!"

Sarah snapped her headphones on and zoned out for the quick flight from Minneapolis to Chicago.

"Finally here!" Sarah said out loud as she walked off her final flight of the day and headed out toward the exit. Though she saw the faces of frustrated travelers around her, she had a spring in her step, excited to be at her final destination. She was familiar with this brief adrenaline rush and knew exhaustion from the day would catch up to her at some point. *I got this!* she thought, giving herself a pep talk as she arrived at the rental car company.

Sarah was able to get her rental car immediately. She familiarized herself with her temporary vehicle, pushing buttons and adjusting the mirrors before she rested her hands on the steering wheel. She mentally prepared herself for the two-and-a-half-hour drive ahead and sighed deeply, feeling the exhaustion of the flip-flopped travel day settle in.

Not familiar with the northern destination, Sarah briefly questioned if getting a hotel room for the night would be a better option. She could grab dinner, sleep off the exhaustion, and hit the road bright and early in the morning. The hotel option left her thoughts just as quickly as it appeared. She took a few deep breaths, gave herself another pep talk, and drove off full of anticipation toward the vacation cottage.

CHAPTER 2

The sun was still hanging around fairly late on this early October evening, which helped guide Sarah along her way. The large trees and fields lining the highway gave her comfort, reminding her of her childhood home in upper New England.

"What beautiful colors!" she said in a brief moment of awed contemplation. "Even with shitty travel mix-ups, there are silver linings."

Sarah yawned and shifted in her seat, trying to stay alert, when she was startled by her GPS telling her to exit the interstate in two miles. She sat up straight as anticipation took over. She wondered if she should use her remaining energy to make a stop at a market. However, her excitement was greater than hunger, so she chose to go directly to the cottage instead.

She drove down the long lake road leading to the rental property, and even with the sun beginning to set she could still catch glimpses of the water between the houses. The beautiful little lake was surrounded by newer homes with large windows, fresh concrete driveways, and light exterior colors. Based on the pictures of her rental cottage, she wondered if its small size with old dark siding and rustic screen porch might appear out of place next to these big homes. She shrugged once again. *Not my concern. It will be perfect for me for the week!*

The GPS interrupted Sarah's thoughts instructing her to turn left in two hundred feet. She could not see the cottage on the other side of the large pine trees, yet she did notice a dangling address sign barely attached to a metal stake. Her smile of excitement was quickly replaced with a frown of concern.

"What the hell?" Sarah wondered.

She drove slowly down the winding driveway as the GPS repeated, "You have arrived at your destination."

"This is not my destination, lady!" she replied sternly to her GPS. The driveway was cracked and full of potholes. Sarah drove as far as she could down the driveway only to reach a flattened yard filled with dirt and the lake just beyond. There was no house to be found!

Sarah rubbed her tired eyes not believing what she was seeing. She reached over to the bag sitting in the passenger seat and pulled out her printed rental contract. With a hand on her hungry and now nervous stomach, her instincts told her something was not right. Still holding the contract, Sarah got out of the car and walked near the lake until she stood exactly where she thought the cottage was supposed to be. She pulled out her phone to call the rental company. "Shit!" she yelled a bit too loudly for her surroundings. "I am in the middle of nowhere. Of course I wouldn't have any service!"

She walked back to the car, shaking her head in disbelief. Confused, she glanced through her rental agreement one more time. *It's gotta be a fricking scam,* she thought, remembering an article she recently read about similar things happening all over Europe. Yet she remained in disbelief it could actually happen in the US, much less in Pleasantville Midwest, USA.

Sarah was overtaken with exhaustion and emotion at the same time. A familiar feeling set in as panic brewed in her pressure-filled chest. After the day she'd had, and the stress of her deadline, she couldn't keep her emotions from boiling over. She kicked the car tires in anger and a stream of obscenities rolled off her tongue in quick succession. With the last word of vulgarity came the flood of tears.

In the midst of her breakdown, a woman walked by with her dog and witnessed the whole episode. With compassionate curiosity, the woman approached Sarah. "Hello, hello."

Sarah, surprised to hear someone talking to her, snapped out of her fit, briefly. "You scared the shit out of me!" She looked at the stranger with rageful yet weary, red eyes.

The woman replied, "I'm so sorry to startle you. I saw you were upset and wondered if I could help. My name is Mary. I live a couple houses down."

Sarah took a deep breath and burst out with sarcastic anger, "Well, Mary, since you live around here, maybe you could tell me about the crook who owns this place. So much for the safe Midwest neighborhood touted in the description." Sarah shook her now-crumbled contract at Mary. "This area is no better than the city I left. Ugh, what a crock of shit!"

Sarah's abrasiveness caught Mary off guard and changed her understanding smile to a scowl. She reciprocated Sarah's insults with a spiteful tongue herself, "Well, young lady, I was going to offer you help, but since you chose to insult my neighborhood, I will be on my way. I am sorry that you appear to be having a very bad day. Hopefully it gets better for you." Mary turned to walk away with a harder than normal tug on her dog's leash. "Let's go, Tito! We aren't needed here." They continued down the driveway.

Sarah rolled her eyes in frustration with herself and walked quickly after Mary. "I am such an idiot!" Sarah said as she was reminded of the bitchy little child she used to be when things didn't go her way. "Please wait. Please, I am so sorry. I lost my temper. I didn't mean to take my anger out on you. Please, stop." Sarah slowed her walk as she caught up to Mary. "I can explain!"

Mary turned and said, "No need to explain. I hope your evening turns around." She continued walking.

"Please. I'm sorry. Please just let me explain. I think I could use your help."

Sarah reached out her hand as if to touch Mary's arm while Mary stopped and glanced at her with an expression that said, Do not touch me.

Sarah looked at Mary with her droopy eyes and pleaded, "I understand you were caught off guard with my outburst, but I could really use some help. May I please ask you a couple of questions?"

Sighing, Mary turned around and replied with bitter sarcasm, "Are you sure you want to ask me questions? I could be a crook in this unsafe neighborhood." Mary shook her head as her glance fell toward the ground. She then took a deep breath and placed her hand on her chest to look up at Sarah with a small smirk. "Now I should be the one to apologize. That was rude. I am sorry. How about we start again?"

Sarah nodded in agreement.

"My name is Mary, and this is my dog, Tito. We live a couple of houses down. Is there anything that we can help you with?"

Sarah, sighing with relief, said, "My name is Sarah. I rented a cottage that, according to this contract," shaking the crumbled piece of paper, "was supposed to be right there." She pointed to the dirt by the lake.

Mary's eyes were wide with shock as she responded, "Are you kidding me? There hasn't been a house on this property for at least five years. There must be a mistake. Maybe the address was wrong. Do you mind if I look at the contract?"

Sarah showed Mary the rental contract, and they both compared the address number on the dangling sign with that on the contract. Mary pointed to the letterhead logo and said, "I have never heard of this company, but it looks legit."

Sarah asked her if she knew the person who owned that property, and Mary explained she'd never met her. However, she'd heard the owner inherited the prior house and lot from family.

"I believe someone mentioned she lives in New Mexico," Mary explained. "I was told she wanted to build her retirement home here, but other than a lawn service cutting grass in the summer, nothing has been done to this place since the house was torn down years ago." Mary glanced at the contract once again, searching for the owner's name, but could only find the name of the rental company and a phone number. "I'm sure there was a simple mix-up. Maybe you should give them a call." She handed the paper back to Sarah.

Sarah replied, "I tried before but couldn't get any cell service out here."

"Yeah, there are spotty areas around here. You're welcome to use my phone if you'd like. It generally comes in fine." Mary removed her phone from her jacket pocket and offered it to Sarah.

"Thank you. I'll call right now." Sarah stepped away from Mary and Tito to make the call. She dialed the number and was immediately greeted with a message, "This number has been disconnected and no longer in service." She dialed again and heard the same message. Without any words, tears streamed down Sarah's face, only this time she didn't feel anger, just defeat. "I am such a fool. I booked this place quickly and didn't think to cross-reference like I usually do when traveling."

The sun was beginning to set, so she had to do something soon. She looked at Mary's compassionate expression and said, "I guess I have to cut my losses and forget about my writer's retreat. I need to find a hotel for the night and book a flight back to Boston in the morning. My book's deadline is quickly approaching in six days and, unfortunately, I'm behind with my edits from this cottage mishap along with my derailed travel day. I'll have to worry about the rental issue when I get back home."

Mary's sympathetic grin reminded Sarah of her own mom as she said, "I'm sorry you've had to go through all of this. It sounds like you are under a tight timeline. Listen, Sarah, I know we just met, yet for some reason my gut is telling me you are a good person. Honestly, you remind me a bit of my own daughter. If you'd like, you could come to my house and make arrangements for a hotel and return flight. It may be easier with the Wi-Fi rather than trying to deal with spotty cell service using your phone."

Mary then mentioned she had dinner in the slow cooker and would be happy to make Sarah a plate before she went to the hotel. Sarah, though apprehensive from the kindness of this stranger, decided her extreme hunger would win over the concern of safety from entering a stranger's home.

Upon walking through the front door, Sarah realized just how tense she had been when her shoulders finally relaxed from the immediate feeling of comfort she felt in Mary's home. Mesmerized, she stared out at the lake through the large east-facing window. "Wow, what a beautiful view!" She walked toward the window with her eyes locked on the lake. "It's hard to take my eyes off the lake."

"Thank you. The view never gets old!" Mary said.

Sarah glanced away briefly to ask Mary if she could use the restroom.

"Not a problem at all, Sarah. It's right down the hall." Mary pointed her in the direction and asked, "Would you like something to drink? Water, wine?"

"That sounds great! I'd take both if that's okay. Thank you!"

Sarah returned and joined Mary at the small wet bar. Mary handed her the glass of wine as Sarah looked around and said, "I like this room. It feels like the lake is so close through those big windows. And the reflection of the trees with their fall colors is breathtaking."

"Thanks, Sarah!"

Sarah continued, "Do you spend most of your time in this room?"

Mary replied, "We really do. We initially designed the room to be a porch, but at the last minute decided to make it a four seasons room so we could enjoy the view all year long rather than just when the weather was nice."

Sitting down, Sarah felt the calming effects of the wine setting in, so she decided to wait until after dinner to plan her next steps. "What a day! Mary, I am sorry again for how I acted earlier. You had to think I was quite the brat."

Mary replied, "I am a bit ashamed of my reaction as well. I'm happy we could move past that and start again. Sarah, I'm sorry you stumbled upon some bad luck. After dinner I'd be happy to help you find a decent hotel while you work on your return flight. We'll have you on your way and sleeping off the day in no time."

While Mary was talking, Sarah was trying to hold herself back from inhaling her food. Mary was saying her husband and sons were on a hunting trip in Missouri and her daughter was abroad in London for the semester. "I do appreciate the quiet time in the house, but I usually miss them the minute they walk out the door." A sadness showed in Mary's eyes. "My daughter left a month ago, and although I am excited for her, I miss her so much it hurts."

"Your daughter will never regret the decision to step out of her comfort zone and study abroad!" Sarah expressed as she remembered her abroad travel during college.

The conversation continued after dinner. "So, Sarah, what brought you to our little lake in the first place? Earlier you mentioned something about a writer's retreat and being on a deadline. Are you an author?"

Sarah took her last sip of her wine and then said, "I'm happy to fill you in but wondering if I could pour another glass of this amazing wine first?"

Mary gave Sarah a sideways smirk and said, "Absolutely! Can you pour one for me too?"

CHAPTER 3

With their glasses refilled, the women cleared the table and moved back to the sunroom. Mary took the armchair, which she comfortably sank into, offering Sarah to kick back between two knit pillows on the wide and comfy sofa. Sarah sighed with contentment. "Ah! Mary, you might not get me out of your home. I'm feeling pretty comfortable here."

Mary's raised eyebrows piqued Sarah's intuition. She wondered if Mary actually thought she was serious with that comment. Her defensive response kicked in before she even realized it happened.

"But not to worry. I will be on my way shortly," Sarah offered quickly while standing up from her place on the couch. "I understand your apprehension with my being in your home. Honestly, I should've just found a hotel for myself right away. I appreciate your hospitality, Mary, but I don't need to take up any more of your time." Sarah's glass clinked loudly when she set it on the stone coffee table. She glanced up at Mary and began walking out of the room.

"Wait a minute, Sarah. What just happened here? I thought we were sitting down to chat about your writing," Mary inquired.

"After I made the comment that you might have a hard time getting me out of your home, I thought you had a nervous look on your face. My gut told me I overstayed my welcome." Sarah looked flushed from embarrassment. She glanced at the floor and then up at Mary, "I'm sorry, Mary. I think my exhaustion has made me a bit too sensitive tonight."

"I understand. It's been a long day. I get the same way when I'm tired. My daughter too," Mary reassured her before continuing. "I was looking forward to hearing about your writing. However, if you are too tired to do that, I can help you find a hotel close by so you can get some rest."

"I'm good with chatting a bit longer. I'll make it brief and be on my way," Sarah said still standing, ready to depart.

"I'd love to hear more. Plus, you don't want your wine to go to waste." They both laughed as Mary waved Sarah back into the room.

"Let's see, where do I begin?" Sarah rhetorically asked. "Have you ever felt a strong pull to do something outside your comfort zone, only to be bombarded with self-doubt? A doubt so nagging it discouraged you from even making an attempt?" Mary nodded in agreement, and Sarah continued, "That's how I have felt for years with regard to writing a novel. It's not that I doubted my ability to write, but more that I doubted my ability to carry it through until the end. Writing articles for *Simple Travels* is somewhat easy, as my inspiration is fueled by the vast array of locations I visit. Each article offers a fresh perspective. However, the process is somewhat routine and within my comfort zone. I compare writing these articles to running sprints. They are impactful yet over quickly.

"Writing a book, however, is more of a marathon, where I need to keep a steady pace until the end. I have to keep a great deal of words and thoughts organized for someone with a short attention span like me." They both laughed. "So my doubt was not so much in the writing itself but rather in the process of maintaining interesting content. Does that make sense?"

Mary replied, "I can appreciate the sprint versus marathon analogy. It has to be quite gratifying to write in the form of small, inspirational bursts for your articles. That's a great way to prevent writer's block!"

Sarah replied, "No kidding!"

Mary took a sip of her wine as a slight smile touched her lips. Her eyes seemed to focus on the shelves at the far wall and then darted back to Sarah. "So what finally pushed you into the marathon of writing?"

Sarah replied, "It wasn't one particular thing that pushed me. It was mostly my lifelong love of writing combined with encouragement from friends and family. Plus, the timing seemed right as my social life had been dwindling the past couple of years with many of my friends getting married and having children. And, though my family doesn't agree with me, I don't feel the time is right for me to pursue a relationship yet."

Mary, looking confused, scowled and asked, "Why do you feel it's not the right time to pursue a relationship? Is there ever really a right time?"

Sarah replied, "Good point." With a long pause, Sarah glanced up at the ceiling before continuing her story. "Let me see if I can give some insight as to how and why relationship timing is important to me. Going back more than ten years, when I was in high school, it was more important to attend or plan the next outing than it was to figure out my algebra problems. Therefore, as you can imagine, my grades in high school were not my priority. When it came time to get serious about applying to college, deficiency in my studies caught up to me."

Sarah smirked and then rolled her eyes to signify frustration in her younger self before continuing.

"I dreamed of attending Boston University, but I knew there was no possible way that would happen with the current status of my academics. In addition to that, my high school guidance counselor told me I was not college material." Sarah paused briefly. "Even though that comment hurt, truthfully, it was exactly what I needed to hear to motivate me to kick ass in my future. My dad had a dear friend who worked at the local college, and she was singlehandedly the reason for my acceptance into school, offering me a chance to prove that I was, indeed, college material."

Sarah yawned and then chuckled slightly.

"I'm sorry, Mary. I'm getting tired of hearing myself talk. I need to focus…"

Mary laughed at Sarah's comment and settled back into her chair, sipping her wine.

Sarah continued, "Henry, my ex-boyfriend, and I dated for two years prior to college starting. We had been best friends when we started dating and were fearful we'd mess up our friendship if the relationship didn't work. Well, it didn't work out. We gave it the old college try, no pun intended, but distance between our two colleges won in the end." Sarah's eyes filled with tears as she flashed back to her breakup with Henry. "I can still see his face on that spring day after our freshmen year. We were sitting in his car at the local ice cream drive-in restaurant…"

* * *

"Henry, I know both of us think we want this relationship to work, but you have to be honest and agree it's been tough trying to balance schedules, much less distance. It's not fair to ask you to manage being in a relationship halfway across the country with all you have going on with school and lacrosse. And it's not fair to ask me to travel every other weekend to see you."

Henry replied, "I get it, Sarah. We seem to have this same discussion every other month. The distance has been a challenge for both of us, but don't you think we can figure something out? We have similar visions of our life together. If we let go now, we are taking a chance that we won't be together in the future. What if you start seeing someone new? Sarah, that would drive me crazy, and I know you'd feel the same way if I started dating someone else."

"I understand, Henry, but we are just finishing our freshmen year. Why do we have to let our future be determined by our lives right now? We both have to make decisions based on what is happening now, not what will happen in the future. Plus, Henry, you are living out your dream of playing lacrosse for the school you wanted to be at!" Sarah said, trying to make eye contact with Henry, but he looked away.

She hesitated a moment and then gently turned his face toward her and continued in a soft tone.

"You also know how much it means to me that I finally got into Boston University—a school I've only talked about a zillion times since I met you. I will already be a year behind and will want to dive in right away and meet new friends. I will want to enjoy my own college. I can't do that if I leave on the weekends." Sarah put both hands softly on Henry's cheeks and calmly said, "Henry, this is about both of us and what we want to do to with our lives right now, not three to five years from now."

"So what are you saying, Sarah? Are you breaking up with me?" Henry asked with an angry tone as he pushed her hands from his face. "Just because you got into BU, that means we have to end our relationship? Now your dream is more important than mine! Or is it that you want to go meet some new guys in your 'creative writing class'?" Henry made fingers quotes. "What a joke!" He followed up with a cruel laugh.

Sarah took a deep breath, trying to calm herself down after his belittling comments. "I'm saying maybe we need to step back a bit and focus on ourselves. Focus on making our own dreams come true so we can come together down the road and feel we've achieved what we each set out to do. We have talked about a future, Henry, but I don't think there will be a future together if we force the relationship now."

Sarah noticed Henry's red eyes as she reached over to try and hug him. He gently pushed her away and looked the opposite direction.

They sat quietly for a few minutes before Sarah spoke again. "Henry, I understand you are upset. This isn't easy for me either. I don't want this to end, but this past year was very tough on both of us."

Sarah had seen Henry's anger streak before when things didn't go his way, and truthfully, she had quite the feisty temper herself. At this moment, she was doing everything in her power to stay calm, which wasn't easy when he blurted out, "Well, Sarah, as far as I'm concerned, I think it's a waste of time and money for you even to pursue a college degree. You know you aren't cut out for college anyway. Plus, we both know you're going to stay at home once we're married and have kids. It's what we talked about… remember?" Henry tilted his head to the side with a cocky grin.

Finally feeling her blood boiling, Sarah retaliated with a louder tone and said, "Henry, you have no right to put me down like that. I worked so hard this year and was finally accepted into BU because of it. I deserve to pursue a degree as much as you do! Plus, if you keep being such an asshole, I won't be marrying you or having your children!" Sarah took a few deep breaths, looked out the passenger window and said quieter now, "Please take me home! I think we know this won't go anywhere tonight with both of our tempers flared."

* * *

Sarah looked at Mary with a fire in her eyes and said, "I think I need a little bit more wine! I get a little fired up when I think of that night."

Mary grabbed the bottle and poured Sarah more wine while offering support. "I can see you're upset, Sarah. It's never easy to relive such a painful experience, even if it was long ago."

After taking a good swig of her wine, Sarah said, "Thanks, Mary. In a way, it seems like yesterday."

"Well, did the prince ever come around again?"

Sarah continued with the story, "It took a few days before we spoke again after our break-up and agreed, in a civilized manner, that we were better off going our separate ways. Then we didn't speak again for a year until we saw each other out at a summer party in our hometown. We talked for hours, which brought up old feelings again. At that time, I was living in Boston full time and just up for the weekend. Henry was only in town for a short time and had to go back for off-season workouts. We decided not to confuse things again by rekindling the flame. However, we enjoyed reconnecting."

"So no fairytale ending?" Mary asked.

"Not exactly," Sarah replied. "Trust me, Mary. I am a closet romantic, so I wanted nothing more than to have a fairytale ending. But I had other personal and professional dreams I wanted to accomplish first. I felt, and continue to feel, strongly about finding my sense of self first. I need to discover the purpose for my own existence before I can share my existence with a man, much less children."

Mary's expression softened. "Do you think things need to fall in a certain order before you discover your life's purpose?"

"Yes, that's exactly how I see it!" Sarah exclaimed before standing up. "I could go on about this topic, but getting back to your original questions about my book… basically the timing was right and I was up for the challenge of the proverbial marathon of writing! I decided to write my own love story and use some of my favorite places around the world as the backdrop. Now I just have to see if my publisher will give me a thumbs up for the final manuscript, which is due in six days."

Mary stood up as well and walked with Sarah into the kitchen. "Well, I bet your publisher will give you a double thumbs up!" They both laughed again and, in the moment of silence, simultaneously finished their wine.

CHAPTER 4

They continued their conversation about Sarah's book while they walked into the kitchen. After a brief pause, Sarah looked at her watch and stood straight up. "Oh my lord, Mary, I didn't realize how late it's gotten. I've been sitting here babbling about myself like a self-centered twirp. I feel bad for taking over your Saturday night."

"Not a problem, Sarah. I didn't have any particular plans on the docket for tonight. Tito and I have the week to ourselves, so it was nice to have some company for dinner."

Silence filled the air while the ladies busied themselves with washing the few dishes they used for dinner. Sarah was silently reflecting on the conversation they just had when she felt a twinge of worry set in about her deadline and the fact she had made zero progress all day. *I have to get going.*

Sarah carefully set down her last dish and said, "I think it's time I get my next twelve hours figured out. I'm feeling the stress of unfinished edits setting in." Sarah opened her laptop, and asked Mary for her Wi-Fi password.

Mary put the dishes back in the cabinet while offering Sarah the password. She then turned around quickly and walked over to Sarah. "This may sound like a crazy offer, seeing we are complete strangers, but you are welcome to stay here for the night rather than going to a hotel. I assume you aren't an evil person, or Tito would've barked like a mad dog when you came into his abode."

Sarah replied, "Mary, that is so nice of you, but I can't put you out any more than I already have."

Mary hung the towel on the dishwasher handle and walked toward the front door. "It's up to you. I won't try and convince you, but the offer is open if you'd like. You could stay in my daughter's room upstairs and wouldn't bother me a bit." Mary opened the door and shouted, "Tito! Time to go outside!"

Sarah was still at the island, staring at her computer. "Thanks, Mary. I can't tell you how much I appreciate your hospitality. I'll get this figured out and be out of your hair." Sarah's mood went from content to frustrated as she angrily tapped away on her keyboard. "I still can't believe I was scammed out of the rental cottage. Ugh, it makes me so angry!"

Mary, back at the island, yawned and shook her head. "I hate that something like this could happen in my neighborhood. I need to ask around, maybe others know more about that property. For all I know, the owner could be behind the whole thing." Mary shrugged and started wiping the counters.

"There has to be a logical explanation," Sarah said and then looked at Mary. "Do you mind if I use the restroom?"

Mary, scratching away a sticky spot on the counter, didn't glance up. "Help yourself, dear!"

On her way to the restroom, Sarah noticed a small room off the kitchen that she didn't see earlier. A reflection from something hanging on the wall caught her eye. Now out of Mary's sight, Sarah curiously stopped. She looked at the tiny space that appeared to be a closet. *What is this room?* Sarah wondered as she quietly peeked her head inside. It looked like some pictures were framed on the wall. The room was dark so she couldn't see what they were. Sarah, curious about the tiny space, slid her hand along the wall in search of the light switch. Though nervous about being caught, when Sarah didn't find the light switch, she pushed her head further inside the room.

"Boo!" Mary said as she walked up behind Sarah.

"Oh my gosh, you scared the shit out of me!"

Mary laughed while Sarah backed out of the small room before having the chance to see what was hanging on the wall. "It's easy to get confused with the many doors down this hall. The bathroom is one more over." Mary casually pointed.

"Yes, I got confused," Sarah said, feeling relieved.

A few minutes later, Sarah slid onto the chair at the kitchen island and stared at her own reflection in the screen of her laptop. She tapped her foot as Mary, sitting in the sunroom just off the kitchen, nestled in her armchair and flipped through pages of a catalog. Finally, Sarah could no longer contain it: "Mary, I have to be honest with you. I knew that room wasn't the bathroom back there. When I was walking by something hanging on the wall caught my eye. I wanted to see what it was, so I was just being nosy. Here you let a stranger into your home and then I go snooping around."

Mary laughed while setting down her book. "Sarah, no worries at all. Honestly people do confuse the two rooms quite often. I appreciate your honesty, though." Mary paused and set her glasses on top of her book before explaining. "The first room down the hall used to be a pantry but has become my little office. With the kids mostly out of the house, we don't need so much food. Therefore, I was able to create a space to call my own. Even if it meant giving up some extra storage for cookies and chips."

Mary, seeming quite lighthearted about the whole thing, laughed and gestured invitingly with wide-open arms. "As long as you don't steal anything, you are welcome to look around the house as much as you'd like."

Sarah's quick temper set in, coupled with embarrassment. "Thank you, but now, feeling like a free loader and a fool, I need to get out of your home." With her red face and quick movements, she packed up her computer in haste and grabbed her purse. Sarah's tone mimicked her earlier reaction when she first met Mary. "I will just drive back toward the airport tonight and find a hotel along the way. This whole day has been a complete shit show."

Mary remained calm and said, "Sarah, I understand you are worn out, but please don't be upset about looking around. It's not a big deal. Truly, I have nothing to hide. I also enjoyed meeting you today, so I hope you don't think the entire day was a—what did you call it? Shit show."

Sarah looked down with a sheepish expression and said, "You really are a nice person, Mary. I've heard people from the Midwest were so friendly, but now I have proof!"

"Thanks, Sarah! I am just the product of my upbringing. Living here my whole life, Midwest values are all I know." After a brief silence, Mary continued, "I understand you wanting your own space, but know the offer stands for you to spend the night if you choose."

Standing by the front door with her hand on the door knob, Sarah replied, "Though that sounds great, especially now that it's gotten so dark, I have overstayed my welcome and should be on my way. Thank you once again for dinner, wine, and excellent conversation."

Mary stood in the front foyer, squatting down to pet Tito. "You're welcome on dinner and such. I enjoyed the company."

Sarah smiled and started walking outside with Mary and Tito following a few steps behind.

Sarah surprised herself when she offered to hug Mary. "Wow, Mary, you must have a special way about you, because I have never been an initiator of hugs. I guess you draw out my soft side."

Mary smiled and offered an additional hug before wishing her safe travels back home. "And good luck with your final manuscript. I will keep an eye on the bestsellers list!"

Sarah now sat in the driver's seat. "Wouldn't that be fun!" She shut the door and rolled down the window to wave goodbye to Mary as she walked back toward the house. "Thank you again!" Sarah shouted.

Sarah started the car at the same time she saw her phone light up next to her. "Shit!" she said, realizing she left her phone in the car the whole night. She now had twenty texts and ten missed calls all from her mom. To reduce further panic from her mother, she dialed her immediately.

CHAPTER 5

―

Mary watched Sarah pull away before briskly walking into her little office. She opened up her computer and started typing as fast as her fingers allowed. Catching Tito staring at her from the corner of her eye, she said, "Tito, I promise I'll take you for a walk shortly, but I have to get these snippets saved before I forget. I am definitely adding this scenario to my next book."

Mary, typing away and lost in thought, didn't hear the front door open. Tito left her side, per normal, when someone was at the house, but he didn't bark, so she continued. Startled by a voice, Mary snapped back to reality once again. Her heart beating faster, she stopped typing so she could listen. "Tito! Come here!" she raised her voice to yell once again. "Tito!"

Tito came running to Mary's side as she looked up to see the shadow of a figure walking down the hall. Her heart beat faster, and her body was paralyzed with nervousness. "Mary," she heard her name. And there, standing in her office doorway, was Sarah, sobbing.

"Oh my Lord, Sarah, you scared me! What happened? You couldn't have been gone more than twenty minutes. Is everything okay with your mom and your family?" Mary asked as she walked closer to Sarah.

Sarah spoke with a rapid pace, "Oh gosh, yes, everything is good now, but my mom was in full-on panic mode because I wasn't communicating like usual. Anyway, I called her when I left your house to fill her in on the whirlwind day and missed the GPS signaling a turn onto the freeway. I went eight miles in the wrong direction before I realized I missed my turn. I told my mom what happened and asked if I could call her back when I corrected my route. Once I hung up with her, I turned around and couldn't help the tears from falling. The day has officially caught up with me, and I don't think I should be driving a minute longer." Pausing to catch her breath, Sarah continued, "Could I please take you up on the offer to spend the night?"

"Absolutely, Sarah! I'm happy you felt comfortable enough to come back," Mary offered while giving Sarah a hug.

Sarah closed her eyes and felt herself relax into the motherly hug for a moment. When she opened her eyes, slowly releasing herself from Mary's embrace, she looked over Mary's shoulder and saw the reflection that caught her eye earlier. There, on the wall, hung three glass frames holding what looked like posters. In an instant she realized they weren't posters at all. They were enlarged book covers. Very familiar looking book covers. Releasing from Mary's hug, Sarah looked at her with wide eyes as if she just hit the jackpot. She was in awe.

Walking toward the framed pieces, Sarah was hit with a brief memory of when she picked up Mary's first book sitting on her mom's nightstand. She was intrigued, once again, by the silhouette of the mystique mountains. She pointed to the pictures and looked back at Mary, saying, "Mary Katherine Thomas! *Four Palms, Four Mountains* series! Are you *the* Mary Katherine Thomas?"

Mary smirked and politely replied, "That would be me! You caught me!"

"Are you kidding me! I *love* your books! I have read the *Four Palms, Four Mountains* series several times! Oh my gosh, wait until my mom hears that I met frickin' Mary Katherine Thomas." Sarah, now less sleepy, just shook her head in disbelief. "Wow! This is unbelievable! You have been my inspiration for years and one of my favorite authors of all time! I can't believe I am standing right here with Mary Katherine Thomas! I've always been a believer of divine intervention, but now I'm convinced of it!"

"Okay, okay, okay, please stop. You're embarrassing me." Mary blushed while waving her hands in front of her face, shaking her head.

"Seriously, Mary, I have this book in the car with me right now!" Sarah pointed to the first poster in the row with continued excitement in her voice. "I pack at least one of your books every time I travel!"

Mary joined Sarah standing next to the framed posters on the wall and pointed to the cover from her first book. "This one is probably older than you. I'm honored you still have it!"

Sarah's captivated tone continued. "Are you kidding me? I know all three of the stories by heart at this point. You have always been an inspiration to me, and now you're right here. Right in front of me. Oh my gosh, I'm standing in your house!"

Mary laughed modestly and then walked away from the wall of framed posters toward her desk as she humbly said, "I love the accolades, but it's been a long time since those books were published. Almost twenty-one years already since the last one. The time has flown by." Mary looked out the window at the dark sky. "Sarah, I am truly honored to hear your excitement, yet I don't even feel like that same woman anymore. That was a lifetime ago."

Sarah's excitement calmed as Mary became melancholy. "Why did you stop writing? You are so talented, and your story lines are unique. I kept waiting for a new release."

Mary took a deep breath and then invited Sarah to sit down by gesturing her toward the cushiony stool next to the desk. "Well, you remember how you talked about an order to your life? How you wanted to have your career now and family when the time was right? I had a similar plan for career first and then family later. However, God had a different plan! We were twenty-five and were comfortable with the DINK label people gave us."

Sarah realized her poor posture and rolled her shoulders back while frowning slightly in confusion. "What is a DINK label?"

Mary continued, "I suppose that term alone ages me." They both laughed. "It stands for double income no kids. We were married at twenty-three and by twenty-five I had already published the first novel in my series. The second novel was completed quicker, only nine months after my first one was on the market, because the publishing process was more familiar."

Mary paused to catch her breath before adding more.

"Before Frank and I got married, I worked full time for a small advertising agency, and Frank was employed in finance with a local corporation. We were married young, but plenty our age were doing the same, so it seemed like a natural progression. Many even started families right away."

Sarah interrupted, "Wait! Did you say you were married at twenty-three? That seems so young! Is that a Midwest thing to marry young?"

"I guess you could say that was the case for us along with some of our family and friends. It didn't seem young at the time because we just carried on with our same youthful fun, only as a married couple." Mary smiled and twirled her glasses. "Though it was our plan to wait until at least twenty-eight to start a family, Frank and I were thrilled beyond measure to see the two pink lines on that beautiful spring morning! We were twenty-five when sweet Billy was born. We were smitten over him from day one." Mary, with a peaceful glow, looked up at Sarah with a content sparkle in her eyes.

Sarah noticed a brief change in Mary's expression. As if she wore motherhood with a prideful expression different than when she spoke of her writing. Sarah saw a softening in Mary's shoulders and around her eyes as she spoke about her child.

After briefly losing herself in thought, Sarah inquired, "Based on the age you started your family, you continued your writing into motherhood. Did you also continue your work at the ad agency? My sisters and many of my girlfriends tried to keep their careers, but most gave them up to be full-time moms. I'm not sure I have that in me."

Mary sighed while leaning back in her desk chair. With her glasses resting in her lap, she said, "Being a stay-at-home mom isn't for everyone, Sarah. Though it works for some women, I believe obligation will only create a sense of animosity. No woman, or man, for that matter, should feel obligated to do something just because that's how it's been done before."

Mary smirked and then leaned her elbows back on the desk. Her face offered a straight expression as she circled the conversation back to Sarah's previous question.

"Let's see. Where did we leave off? Oh yes, after maternity leave, I changed to part time at the agency to be home more with Billy. That was way before the remote capabilities of today, or I may have stayed on full time. I loved being a mom and part-time career woman, but I felt I still needed more. Therefore, I began the process of writing book number three. It took me a little bit longer, but fortunately it was published just before the twins were born."

Mary stood up and started walking toward the door. Sarah followed her lead while Mary finished her story.

"I stepped out of the work world on the day the twins were born and haven't officially been back since. Baby Frankie came along three years after the twins, so we had a full house."

Mary sighed and started walking upstairs.

"Sarah, I am so sorry, my answer was very longwinded. To be honest, I am currently trying to write again but having the damnedest time focusing on a story line. My confidence is shaky from being away for so long. And it doesn't help that I'm a bit of a perfectionist and leery I may have lost what it takes to be a successful author in today's world." Mary raised one side of her mouth to show an expression of wonder and uncertainty.

"Mary, you are remarkable! I have known you for all of four hours yet feel I've known you my whole life! Listening to you tell your story, it's as if you are reading it from the pages of your book. You speak similar to how you write. You definitely have what it takes to be an author in our modern world!" Sarah enthusiastically encouraged. "Thank you for sharing your story with me. I remember hearing that you had a family but held out hope you'd still release more books."

Mary walked with Sarah to Elizabeth's room, showing her where she could find towels, a phone charger, and a space to put her clothes.

Sarah looked around the spacious, bright room, let out a deep sigh, and said, "Thank you, Mary. I will book my flight now before I fall asleep. Hopefully I am able to get on an early plane and won't have to deal with crazy delays again. As you understand better than anyone, I can't delay my writing any longer. A deadline is a deadline! Goodnight, Mary!"

"Goodnight, Sarah. I'll have coffee waiting for you in the morning. Sleep well!"

Sarah took a deep breath while she sat slowly on the end of the bed. Even though it was late on the East Coast, she knew she owed her mom a return call to update her on the change of plans.

"Mom, I understand this whole thing sounds crazy! I don't blame you one bit for your concern, but please trust me. I'm fine. Besides the stress of the rental cottage and travel disruptions, it's actually been a nice night. And Mary seems like a wonderful woman. Her husband and family are all away this week, so I will be staying in her daughter's room," Sarah reassured.

Sarah's mom questioned, "What is the room like? Is there a lock on the door? Ugh, Sarah, I do trust you, but I worry so much. It's just what I do. You know that."

"I get it, Mom. Please know that I'll be fine and will be back tomorrow. If it makes you feel better, I'll call first thing in the morning on my way to the airport."

Sarah concluded the call while still sitting on the end of the bed. She shook her head thinking of the ironic twists of meeting Mary. With a smile on her face, Sarah flopped back onto the bed. *What are the chances?* was her last thought of the night.

CHAPTER 6

Through Sarah's various travels, she was no stranger to waking up to unfamiliar sounds and surroundings. From the bliss of waves hitting the shore in her cave-style room in Greece to tranquil chirping birds from the clear bubble in Iceland, she was seasoned in sights and sounds from around the world, yet this morning was a first for her. She was jolted awake from a loud crack of thunder as close as the neighbor's house followed by a wind gust she was certain would break the bedroom window. "Holy shit!" Sarah said as she sat straight up in bed. "I'm awake now!"

Sarah tossed the covers off Elizabeth's bed and without hesitation stepped toward the window. The lake looked angry this morning. Even for its small size, it had rushing white capped waves. *It's going to be that kind of a day,* Sarah thought as she quickly got dressed. With her heart still pounding from the urgency of the storm sounds, she hurried downstairs to see what was going on.

Noticing Mary contently working in her little office, Sarah disguised her adrenaline rush with a cheery greeting while leaning against the doorway. "Good morning, Mary. Wow! That thunder was quite the wakeup call!"

Mary looked up from her computer with a smile, removed her glasses, and got up to offer Sarah some assistance. "Good morning, Sarah. I hope you slept okay before the storm woke you. That was quite the house rattling thunder!"

Sarah replied as the two walked into the kitchen. "No kidding, but I slept better than I have in years up until that point. I think the exhaustion combined with wine provided the perfect sleep elixir." She smiled at Mary and continued, "But the smell of coffee and cinnamon rolls has a way of calming the nerves back down."

"Isn't that the truth. Please help yourself!" Mary said while offering Sarah a mug.

"Thank you." Sarah took the mug, but her attention was subtly drawn toward the lake. "Geez, even with the ugly weather outside, this view is still beautiful, Mary! It's got to be so nice to look at water every day."

"This little lake does offer a sense of peace, even amidst this chaos." Mary's open-faced hand pointed toward the lake. Both woman laughed as Sarah, holding the coffee pot, began filling her mug. "I am looking forward to this cup of goodness."

Sarah sipped her steaming coffee, noticing Mary's calm expression was now showing concern. Sarah gently set her mug on the island while Mary offered her a cinnamon roll on one of the red-white-and-blue ceramic plates. "Is everything okay, Mary? You look concerned."

"After the day you had yesterday, Sarah, I don't want to give you more bad news, but it looks like these storms are just the beginning of a long line of bad weather in the forecast for today as well as tonight. The news mentioned flights were being canceled all over the Midwest. I'm surprised you didn't hear from your airline."

Sarah gave Mary a look of exasperation and said, "Are you serious? I didn't hear anything from the airline yet, although now that I think of it, I shot out of bed so quickly I didn't even think to check my phone. I'll run upstairs real quick to see if there's something about my flight."

Damn it! she thought as she saw the notification on her locked screen. She paused briefly being distracted by the turbulent lake and walked back down to share the news with Mary.

"Yep, sure enough, you were right! My flight has been canceled! But no notification of a reschedule yet."

The news deflated her, but Sarah didn't show it. She took a deep breath, gathered her thoughts, and walked back to her place at the island. She didn't want Mary to think she was in a hurry to rush out, yet in her mind Sarah knew the delay would put her even further behind with her writing.

Sarah set down her phone next to her plate, reaching for her mug and looking at Mary. "So much for a tranquil writer's retreat. Maybe someone is trying to teach me a lesson. Oh well, it will all work out! I'm wondering if I should start making my way toward the airport just in case the weather breaks. I could always fly standby and do my writing while waiting at the airport."

Mary hesitated before replying, "I certainly don't want to tell you what to do, but your car may not be the safest place to be today. The weatherman said clusters of pop-up tornados have been coming across the country with this system. I understand you'd rather just be on your way, but know you're welcome to stay here until the storm clears."

Sarah held her mug in both hands, pondering her predicament when her thoughts were interrupted by the high-pitched beeping on the TV. She turned to look while a computerized voice announced, "This is an emergency alert system. The national weather service has issued a thunderstorm warning for the following counties…"

Sarah asked Mary, "Are we in one of those counties?" Mary nodded.

"Well, that might make my decision for me. I guess I'll wait out this next round of storms and see if the airline reschedules my flight for me."

"Not a problem! Best to be safe. I wouldn't want my kids on the road in this stuff," Mary graciously offered.

Though frustrated, Sarah accepted the situation. "Thank you! I guess I don't need to finish my breakfast in such a hurry now."

Mary smiled back and asked, "On that note, would you like a refill on coffee?" Hesitating for a couple moments, Mary continued, "Maybe it will end up being a good day for both of us to get some writing done. Feel free to settle back into Elizabeth's room so you have a quiet place to focus."

Sarah replied, "If you don't mind, I think I will do that."

The thunderstorm came and went, followed by rain and strong wind. Sarah sighed a breath of relief after booking a seat on the last flight out of Chicago for the day. That would give her almost a half-day of writing before she headed out. *Not ideal, but I can make it work.* She opened her manuscript and began scanning through her editor's notes on chapter 8. *Thirteen chapters to go,* she thought.

Being Sarah's first book, and the perfectionist that she was, her original plan was to leave plenty of time to edit and re-edit until the story line flowed as smoothly as possible. She knew she left some extra time in her schedule for workouts and mental down time. *If I have to give that up to feel complete, so be it!* she thought, trying to outsmart her frustration.

She was in a zone! A few hours had passed while she worked undisturbed. She took a quick break to stand up and stretch. With her arms above her head, she glanced at her watch and was surprised how fast the time had gone. *Only an hour left before I have to hit the road.*

With her hands resting on her hips, Sarah looked at the wind whipping the trees in the yard and could see the white capped waves creating a small layer of foam on the shoreline. *What a peaceful home, even during this crazy weather.*

Sarah sat back down to put the last edits in for the day when her phone buzzed with a notification. *It's just a text message. I'll check in a few minutes.* She went back to type, but then an unfamiliar, blaring alert came across her phone. She glanced down and read it was an emergency alert: *Tornado Warning.* "Shit!" Sarah said, grabbing her phone and walking quickly downstairs. Mary was walking toward Sarah with the same alert buzzing on her phone and the TV beeping again in the background.

"Well, just when we thought we were in the clear, this day got even more interesting!" Mary said.

With a slight stutter of nervousness Sarah asked, "Mary, what do we have to do for a tornado warning?"

Mary calmly said, "It's okay, Sarah. We usually go to the basement for precaution, but we haven't had tornados in this area in years. Maybe grab your things just in case. Based on the radar this should be over quickly."

Jogging up the stairs, Sarah remembered she had a buzz on her phone before the weather alert. She looked down to see the airline had once again canceled her flight. "Holy shit, could this day get any worse?" she said while quickly packing up her computer and grabbing her bag.

The ladies retreated to the finished area of the basement, which was another cozy space with video games, a sectional couch, and a pizza oven. It appeared like a perfect place for Mary's kids to hang out. Sarah looked around and immediately felt she could be occupied for hours in that room while sheltering from the storm.

Mary sat on the couch and used the remote to turn on the same TV channel that was on upstairs. She snuggled Tito close and said, "I'm not a fan of storms. As a mom, I got really good at pretending I was calm, but inside I'm usually as nervous as the kids. I remember being young and hiding in my parents' basement. I'd carry every personal belonging I could downstairs while my older siblings would sit in the kitchen, cooking pizza and waiting it out. I'd get so worried about them and a little angry too." They both chuckled.

They sat in silence with Tito between them on the couch and looked at the TV blinking and beeping over again with emergency messages. "What county did you say we are in again?" Sarah asked.

Mary replied while pointing at the TV, "The one that is just about to get hit with that dark red blob on the radar." Sarah looked at Mary's frown of concern and started to feel nervous as well. They sat quietly for what seemed like an eternity but was only a few minutes, listening to the weatherman advising people to take shelter.

Sarah realized she was holding her breath with worry when the lights flickered and then went off completely. The small windows in the basement gave off a little light, but it was hard to see or even hear much outside. With concern, she said, "The house is so quiet. It's almost eerily quiet. Maybe it skipped us."

Mary looked at Sarah and said, "Sarah, you stay down here with Tito. I'm going to run upstairs for a minute."

"Wait, why?" Sarah nervously asked.

"It's okay, I just want to check on our generator. I'll be right back down." Mary handed her a flashlight. "Use this if it makes you feel better."

Sarah noticed the natural light from the windows being replaced with darkness and flipped on the flashlight. She sat close to Tito, now in silence. She remembered back to a stormy night when she was around sixteen, alone at the house while her parents were out of town for a business dinner. She prayed her parents would walk in the door at any second as she heard the wind whipping outside. Just as she remembered her relief when her parents came home that stormy night, she heard Mary running back down the stairs.

"Sarah," Mary said with a quiver to her voice, "it's gotten so dark out. I'll have to worry about the generator later. I've never seen a sky look that threatening. Right now, we are best to stay put."

At that moment, the lights flickered on, followed by a shearing sound so loud it rumbled the basement ceiling. Then the lights went out again, and a troublesome silence overtook the room.

CHAPTER 7

Trying to distract their thoughts from the storm, Mary asked Sarah some questions. "I know you mentioned that you live in Boston now, but did you grow up in the city as a child?"

Sarah, still nervous about the storm, replied with a shortness, "I grew up in a small town about forty miles north of the city but moved to Boston for my sophomore year in college and have been there ever since." Sarah stopped abruptly and changed her attention back to the storm. "Are you sure we are safe right now? I feel like we should be doing something other than just sitting here."

Mary put her hand on Sarah's arm and reassured her they couldn't do anything more than waiting out the storm where they were at. Mary redirected the conversation back to Sarah's story of growing up.

Sarah smiled slightly, feeling more at ease with her current situation. "Let's see, back to my childhood. Yes, so I grew up in the greatest neighborhood. My parents still live in my childhood home today, but many of the neighbors have moved. Every time I visit home, though, I feel like I'm walking back in time. I picture how my bedroom used to look with notebooks stacked on the desk, walls full of colorful Post-it notes with motivational quotes and poetry."

A warm smile came across Sarah's face as she let out a little laugh.

"I joked that my first book would be titled *Post-It Notes and Poetry* by Sarah Ann Connelly. I had notebooks full of poems I wrote from the time I was a little girl through high school. I kept them all! I even had short stories about Jack and Sassy, two funny characters who would get into mischief together. From middle school until the time I left for college, I had written at least thirty short stories about those two. I was hoping to one day turn them into a series."

"Now that you have a publisher, you should definitely put Jack and Sassy in print! I'd love to read about them!" said Mary with an excited tone.

Sarah looked sad and replied, "I would, too, but all of my notebooks were lost in a flood shortly after I moved out. I think my mom was more devastated than me when she told me about the flood damage. I brushed it off so she didn't feel bad, but truthfully, I was very sad. Those stories were a positive outlet for me when going through the BS of adolescence."

"Do you think you could jog your memory about some of the story lines?" Mary asked.

Sarah answered, "I guess if I focus long enough, I could recall some of them. I had quite the imagination as a child, so the stories came easy. Unfortunately, I felt the need to hide my story writing in middle school and high school because the imaginative side would've been considered weird or different. Nobody ever wants to be different, especially during those formative years. That being said, I still wrote but didn't let anyone know besides my parents. I used my writing as an escape. One benefit of those years is that they gave me great ideas for story lines."

Mary put her hand softly on Sarah's arm. "That was probably the healthiest outlet for you at the time. Middle school and high school are fun years but can be the most difficult as well. Life-altering moments for many." They sat in dark silence before Mary asked, "If you had to pick one defining moment from your youth, what would it be?"

Sarah replied, "Oh that's an easy one! It was surely defining but not fun to live through. I remember it like it was yesterday. I was in seventh grade. One of my short stories was about this exact topic, only I made it funny in the story. It was quite hurtful in reality.

"It was fall of my seventh grade year when I, along with another friend, were officially phased out of my social group. Though I had plenty of friends in my grade, six of us were in a close-knit group. On the weekends we were always together, and I was generally the point person for social planning. My friends meant everything to me, and I thought we had a solid foundation. We had a safe relationship where we could be ourselves, or so I thought. That came to a screeching halt that day on the playground when Joan and I were outed for being physically different. We thought it was a joke when Tammy and Jane, the bullies of the group, blindsided us."

* * *

"Sarah, when are you ever going to get boobs? You are so flat!" said Jane, one of the more developed seventh-grade girls in the friend group. "You too, Joan! You're flat too! None of the boys like you two. They think you're immature and act weird." Jane looked at Tammy, and they both laughed.

Tammy nodded eagerly, like a player waiting to be let onto the field. "Derek and Andy told Jane, Andrea, Jo, and me if we want to hang with the eighth-grade guys, we shouldn't hang around you girls anymore. They said you aren't like the four of us."

Joan and Sarah looked at each other and laughed when Joan said, "Tammy, what are you talking about? We have hung out together since we were in kindergarten. Those guys are the weird ones. And if they think all that cologne is covering up their bad body odors, well, they're sadly mistaken."

Sarah caught Andrea and Jo laughing, too, so she just brushed it off as a joke and continued, "We don't need to hang around those guys. We have Tim, Brad, and Mike, who want us to hang out. They're a blast!"

Tammy rolled her eyes while looking at Jane. She stepped forward toward Sarah and Joan in the circle of the six friends and said, "Well, we would rather hang around the eighth-grade guys than immature Tim, Brad, and Mike. And the eighth-grade guys don't want you two to come along."

Jane stepped forward to join Tammy in the middle of the circle and said, "Didn't you realize you weren't invited to parties the past two weekends?"

Sarah innocently replied, "We didn't know parties were happening. We thought you all were busy with family gatherings."

Jane snapped back, "Are you kidding me? Do you really think I would spend two weekends with my family? You really are as dumb and immature as you look, Sarah!"

Jane pointed to the other three girls and then herself. "The truth is, the four of us have been going to eighth-grade parties the past two weekends and haven't told you two. We've had a blast and prefer to keep doing things with that group."

Tammy, interrupting Jane with her loud voice, said, "And you two aren't invited! Have fun playing with the boys. We are going to hang with some men! We won't be calling you, so don't call us!"

The four girls started to walk away when Jo turned to look at Sarah and Joan and quietly said, "I'm sorry."

Tammy interrupted, yanked Jo's arm, and said, "Come here and leave those girls alone."

* * *

Sarah, sitting in the shelter of the Midwestern basement, turned to Mary with a grin and said, "And that's when the stories of Jack and Sassy were created. I even added some tales about mean girls as well." Sarah laughed. "I have reflected on that day so many times, and though I lost faith in female friendships from that point on, it was a blessing for my writing habit."

Mary's eyes softened. "I appreciate you sharing with me. It sounds like that was a rough time."

Sarah nodded and said, "It was a tough time, but there were silver linings. Not only did my love for writing grow, but I also believe God used me as an instrument to learn humility. Thankfully our friendship came back around, and to this day Joan, Jo, and I are very close. Though I can't forget that pivotal moment in seventh grade, I have forgiven those girls for the hurt they caused."

With a crack of thunder, Sarah and Mary both were startled back to the reality and the storm going on outside.

CHAPTER 8

It had been only a half hour since Mary and Sarah sheltered in the basement, yet it seemed longer based on their tense muscles. Sarah's stomach started to twinge with worry, and anxiety was making her mind work overtime. *What am I going to do?* She thought about her impending deadline and the uncertainty of her current schedule.

Feeling trapped by the storm and starting to grow impatient, Sarah thought, *I need to get out of here!* She stood up and rolled her shoulders back, trying to chase away her anxious thoughts before she lost her cool. Out of habit, she grabbed her cell phone but already knew there would be no reception, especially in a basement.

"Ugh!" she said as she tossed her phone lightly on the counter near the pizza oven. Since she was unsuccessful with her attempt to wait it out, she snipped at Mary. "Do you have any idea how long we'll be down here? I'm starting to feel my anxiety peak to a new level." Sarah smirked and added a nervous laugh to try and offset her mood.

Mary glanced out the small window to get an idea what was going on outside. "It's hard to hear anything down here, but based on the light coming through the window, maybe the worst part of it has passed. Let's give it a try!" Mary suggested as she walked toward the stairwell. "Tito, come!" Mary slapped her leg signaling the pup to join her, and they cautiously walked upstairs.

Standing at the top of the basement stairs, the ladies looked at the lake.

Mary said, "Well, it's a good sign that the white caps have settled. The lake looks fairly calm." Then Mary, turning to look out the west-facing windows toward the front, demanded, "Oh my lord, Sarah, look out this way!"

Mary slowly opened the front door to let Tito outside when she saw the large tree from the front yard now lying across her driveway.

"Oh no! Look what happened to our big tree!" Mary pointed to the tree with a sullen expression. "That tree was the oldest one left on our property. That makes me so sad."

Sarah, with a questioning look, replied, "I wonder if that happened when we heard that loud sheering noise."

Mary responded with a dazed tone, "That would make sense."

Sarah and Mary walked through the mess of branches and leaves on the way to the fallen tree.

"The tree looks so much bigger lying on the ground," Mary said as Tito came to her side starting to sniff around the large trunk.

Sarah held out her hands, noticing the rain had subsided. Then her vision was distracted by the dark grey sky in the distance.

At the same time, Mary's eyes were drawn in the same direction. She pointed and said, "Sarah, based on that sky, we might be in for another round of storms soon." Mary looked at Sarah with a sad expression and apologized, "Sarah, I am so sorry, but I don't think your car would fit past this tree right now. I so wish Frank and my boys were here to help with this."

Sarah nodded in disbelief of the mess. "Mary, can I help you with anything? I feel so bad that you have to deal with this mess without your boys around."

Mary pulled her cell phone out of her pocket. "Thanks, Sarah. I wish you could help too. I think this problem requires bigger muscles and maybe equipment." Mary looked at her phone. "I'll give my tree guys a quick call." She paused and then rolled her eyes. "Or maybe I won't. It says no service." She showed Sarah the message displayed on her phone. "Do you think it's possible that the storm hit a cell tower?" she asked, even though she already knew the answer.

Sarah could feel her fear brewing in her stomach, yet she knew it would be bratty to focus on herself right now. Mary bent her knees, trying to pick up the tree while a string of obscenities came flowing out of her mouth. Tito ran to Mary's side. Mary's angry, red eyes calmed when Tito licked her cheeks. She fell down onto the still-wet driveway and laughed at the dog so innocently looking for attention.

Sarah witnessed the exchange of mom and pup and surrendered her angst as well. "Leave it to a dog to reassure us that all can be fixed with kisses." Both the woman laughed and watched Tito jump around with good-boy glee. Sarah smiled at Mary and said, "Just think, Mary, it could've been a whole lot worse. That tree could've fallen right on your beautiful house or my car. Instead, it landed perfectly across the driveway without disturbing anything."

Mary smirked and exclaimed, "Great point, Sarah!"

A loud popping noise down the road distracted the ladies from the current tree situation. "Are those sparks coming from that pole?"

Mary grabbed Sarah's arm in a panic. "Sarah, I think we need to go inside."

As the ladies walked inside, the rain started coming down again.

The afternoon storm passed quickly even with no power. They didn't hear any siren warnings in the distance, so the ladies stayed upstairs to wait it out.

Sarah grabbed her computer from her bag and went to the couch in the sunroom. "Well, we may not have power, but at least my laptop battery is charged. I guess I will use this time to go back to editing my manuscript. Times like this, I am thankful I saved updated copies to my desktop."

"Maybe I will grab my computer and join you!" Mary said.

The sound of clicking keyboards was the only noise they heard. Sarah was able to get through another chapter of editing when multiple beeping sounds came from their cell phones. Simultaneously, the ladies picked up the phones from the end tables.

Sarah commented, "It looks like the airline booked me on a flight leaving mid-morning tomorrow. At this point, that is the best possible scenario." She rolled her eyes and continued, "What a crazy twenty-four hours it has been!" Sarah hesitated briefly while staring at her cell phone and looked up over at Mary doing the same thing. "Mary, would there be any chance I could stay another night?"

Mary looked up with a grin. "Girl, I don't think you could get your car out now if you tried." Mary set her phone back down on the small stone table and offered, "Truthfully, Sarah, you're welcome to stay for the rest of the week if that saves you more travel disruption. Plus, it would be nice to have someone with me in the house. It looks like they've forecasted storms for the next few days."

Sarah replied, "Mary, you are too good to me! I'd love to stay but should probably get back to the East Coast before my mom feels the need to come get me herself. She sent a few frantic texts after she saw the weather system coming across the Midwest. That poor woman worries so much. It's got to be hard to be a mom sometimes."

Mary agreed, "Us moms spend most our lives worrying about our children. It's part of the job. I've definitely said plenty of Hail Marys since becoming a mom. I also have a mantra that my own mom used to say, which reminds me to relinquish my control. The big guy upstairs has my back." Mary pointed to the ceiling and continued, "Let go, let God!"

"Good for you to have such a strong faith! I love your mantra. Do you mind if I use that as well?" Sarah asked and paused briefly. "Mary, what did you mean before when you said new forecasted storms? Were you just talking about today and tonight?"

"I wish!" Mary exclaimed. "When our cell service came back, I noticed a weather alert saying storms will continue on and off through the next few days. Maybe we'll get lucky and they will blow over. That happens plenty."

Both women shared a look and then directed their attention back to their computers.

Sarah's fingers were typing feverishly while Mary grabbed her phone again. She pointed to the screen and said, "It looks like the system we got today came up from the southwest. I hope it wasn't that bad in Missouri. Frank and the boys are hunting down there in the middle of nowhere."

Mary paused to take a breath and then waved her phone back and forth.

"Talk about crappy cell service. I hardly hear from those guys when they are down there. It's generally a good thing for them to unplug, especially for Frank, yet there has been many times in the twelve years they've been going to those hunting lodges when I tried to reach them and couldn't. It doesn't help with the worries but does force me to be patient. Again, with the mantra, let go, let God! I guess if they needed something, they'd find a way to reach out."

"And so the mom worries continue!" Sarah said with a sarcastic tone.

"No kidding!" Mary said. "The only time I sleep well is when all my chickens are in the nest. One across the big pond in London and three in the middle of Wide-Open Spaces, USA, equals very little rest for this mama!" Mary pointed to herself.

Sarah continued, "I don't know if I have what it takes to be a mom. Or at least to be a good one. I only have myself to care about right now, and that seems challenging most days."

They both laughed and Mary said, "You will be a great mom, Sarah! Have faith in yourself and the blessings God provides you. I didn't think I would be so good at this mom thing, either, but I'm holding my own and have been for twenty-five years. I couldn't do it without the best parenting partner ever! Frank is an incredible husband, but he's almost an even better dad. He is a true family man!"

Sarah replied, "My mom always thought Henry would be the perfect husband and father. She's a romantic at heart and continues to hold out hope we will get back together, even though he recently got engaged."

CHAPTER 9

Sarah called to update her mom on her latest plan. "Mom, I'm fine! I know it's been very unusual turn of events, but trust me, I am safe. Mary is graciously letting me spend another night in her beautiful home."

"Please tell Mary that I said thank you for keeping my girl safe and sound. She sounds like a wonderful woman, but you've got to admit, it's odd that you're staying with a complete stranger for now a second night," Sarah's mom expressed.

"I understand how it must feel, looking at it from your perspective. Please know I am in good care. It's still unbelievable to me that I am staying with this famous author." Sarah smiled at Mary and continued, "Mom, it would be so cool for you to meet Mary someday. You two have many similarities."

Sarah's mom continued the conversation a bit longer, more reassured that Sarah was going to be fine. "Please call me in the morning, Sarah. I love you!"

"Love you too!"

Sarah set down her phone on the small table while she turned to Mary and said, "Even in the midst of chaos, something about talking to my mom just makes me feel like everything is okay with the world."

Mary glanced up from above her glasses. "It sounds like you have a wonderful relationship with your mom, Sarah!

I had a similar feeling every time I talked to my mom too. The world doesn't seem quite so safe since she passed. I can't explain it, but the feeling is undeniable."

Sarah stood up to stretch and then sat back down again, resting the computer on her lap. "How long has it been since your mom passed away?"

"It's been over five years. Somedays it feels like it was yesterday, while others it feels much longer." Mary put her glasses on the stone table next to her. "After my mom passed, I felt disconnected, like I lost the wind beneath my wings. Learning to fly on my own, without her, has been one of the hardest things I've ever had to do." Mary moved to the edge of her chair. "I have a similar relationship with Elizabeth, and thank God for that girl every single day."

Sarah looked up from her computer screen and acknowledged Mary with a compassionate expression. "If I am blessed to be a mom someday, I hope I have a daughter who grows up to be a friend." She hesitated briefly and continued, "I'm sure you miss your mom. I can't quite imagine learning to live without my mom."

Their conversation was interrupted by the subtle high pitch of Mary's laptop pinging. Mary looked at her screen and commented, "I guess my computer time may be coming to an end. Low battery." Mary put her laptop on the footstool in front of her. "I was hoping our power would've come back on by now. I think I'm going to check on the generator. It was suppose to kick in automatically."

Mary started to walk away when her stomach grumbled loudly enough for both the ladies to hear.

She put her hand on her stomach. "Geez, I didn't realize how hungry I was. Unfortunately, we don't have much food around, so we may have to get creative with dinner tonight.

I'll be back in just a moment." Mary walked down the long back hall.

Sarah laughed at Mary's growling stomach and then realized she was hungry as well. She shrugged off the pangs and continued typing away. From the corner of her eye, she saw Mary's phone light up and vibrate on the table by Mary's chair. She was getting a call from her son, Billy. *Do I answer it?* she wondered. "Mary, your phone is ringing! It's Billy!" Sarah yelled.

"Please answer it!" Mary instructed.

"Hello," Sarah said

"Mom, is that you?" Billy questioned with distraction from voices talking in the background. "Guys, be quiet. I can't hear her!" The background noise quieted.

"No, my name is Sarah. Your mom is in the other room but will be right back."

"Sarah who? Is my mom okay?" He sounded confused and concerned.

"I'm sorry. I'm sure you're confused. My name is Sarah Connelly."

Billy interrupted, "What is going on there? Who are you? Where is my mom?"

Sarah could hear flustered, deep voices in the background. They were asking questions, "Is mom okay? Billy, who are you talking to? Where's mom?"

"Billy? Is that Billy? Your mom is just fine, Billy." Sarah filled him in on the storms the past two days. "There's been some bad storms around here and the power's out right now. She said something about the generator not working and went to check on it. Let me walk down the hall to find her for you."

CHAPTER 9 · 71

"Okay, thanks," Billy replied without conviction. "I'm still confused about who you are and why you're answering her phone."

"Here she is," Sarah said and then handed the phone to Mary.

"Hi, Billy, how are you?" Mary smiled and then mouthed "thank you" to Sarah before turning her attention back to her phone. "It's a long story. No, no, it's fine, honey. Sarah is a wonderful young lady. It's a crazy story, but trust me, I am safe and Sarah is trustworthy. I met her in the neighborhood yesterday," Mary reassured her son.

Sarah could briefly hear Mary trying to calm her son down when she walked back down the hall. Mary's voice trailed off but then got louder again when she turned to follow Sarah toward the kitchen. "...The storms have been so bad. Our big tree by the driveway fell, and we haven't had power for hours."

Sarah glanced at Mary as she took a big gulp of water when she had to squint slightly from the flickering lights coming back to life. "Hallelujah! We finally have power again!" Mary told Billy. "Everything is good here. Please don't worry, Billy. And please tell your dad and brothers that I'm fine. I can hear the concern in their voices. Now tell me, how is the hunt going?"

Sarah left her laptop on the couch but brought her other things back to Elizabeth's room once again. *Geez, it feels like Groundhog Day,* she thought. She felt an ease walking back into familiar surroundings. She looked at the lake and noticed the waves were back to white cap status. *Oh no, here we go again!* She braced herself for more storms.

Not wanting to interrupt Mary's phone call, Sarah sat down on the window seat and, maybe due to boredom or curiosity, texted Henry. *Hey, what's new?*

Within seconds he responded: *Same old :) You?*

Their communication went back and forth a few times. Per usual Sarah quickly felt uncomfortable when Henry's comments were directed back to their past relationship.

Henry: *I really hope I see you soon, Sarah. I'm not giving up yet.*

Every time. It happens, every time. Why do I even reach out to him? Sarah wondered with frustration.

She had moved on from Henry years ago, but for some reason, when she had moments of weakness, she felt the need to check in with him.

Why do I do that? It's not fair. He's in a steady relationship. Why do I feel the need to draw him away from that?

Her mind was spinning with wonder, but the answer was becoming more and more obvious. She was ready to have a person for herself. Henry was the only person who ever filled that long-term boyfriend role. The others were cute and fun but nobody she ever wanted to get serious with. She knew she didn't want Henry, but maybe she was ready for someone.

Sarah, not to impose on Mary's conversation, cautiously headed downstairs to get her computer. Once at the bottom of the stairs she saw Mary pouring two glasses of wine. Mary looked up.

"Oh, there you are! I hope Billy wasn't too mean to you on the phone. He can be pretty protective of me." Mary changed the subject briefly while handing Sarah a large glass of cabernet. "I hope I wasn't too presumptuous, but I poured you a glass of wine. I thought we'd enjoy what peace we have now before the third round of storms sets in."

"Thanks! I like your thought process. When should we expect to brace ourselves for the storm?" Sarah asked.

Mary pointed to the TV and said, "Based on the radar, it says we have about an hour. You may want to charge up your computer and phone just in case we lose power again. These storms are crazy! I can't tell you the last time we had consecutive strong storms around here."

"We will become pros at handling them after this. Who knows, maybe you can add snippets of the past day in your next novel," Sarah said.

"Great minds think alike! I was just thinking that," Mary replied with excitement.

She pulled some food from the fridge to prep a quick dinner while she filled Sarah in on her conversation with Billy.

"He calmed down after a bit and told me they've also had some bad storms and may not be able to hunt tomorrow if the rain continues." Mary walked in circles around the island gathering chips and salsa from the pantry. "Wait, what was I saying again? I can be such a scatter-brain." She laughed and continued, "Oh that's right, the boys. It sounds like there's already some flooding in the fields. Billy was pretty bummed out but holding on to hope the storms will lessen as they get closer. I talked to Frank for a bit, too, and then lost our cell connection. That happens sometimes, and then we just end up texting instead."

"Hopefully they are able to get more hunting in. From what you said, they've been doing this for many years. It's challenging enough to keep traditions going from year to year, so when it does work out, the last thing anyone wants is disruption of any kind," Sarah commented.

Mary replied, "Yeah it is getting harder to find the time each year because the boys are at difference stages in their lives, but from what they tell me, it's worth the schedule juggling to make it happen. I know they enjoy the thrill of the hunt and expressing their manly men sides at the hunting lodge." Both ladies laughed.

"Billy sounded genuinely concerned about you on the phone. It was sweet, yet I felt like he thought I was a danger to you. It would be interesting to meet him in person someday. I wonder if he'd still view me as a possible danger," Sarah expressed and then laughed at the thought of their interaction.

Mary commented, "Yep, that's my Billy! He's quite amazing, if I do say so myself. All four of my kiddos are amazing, but I guess I'm a bit biased." Mary's smile lit up her whole face when she spoke about her family. She had positive descriptions about each of them: Billy, magnetic, happy personality. Elizabeth, lively, thoughtful, and driven. Scotty, witty, secure in himself, and funny. And Frankie, the youngest, sweet guy, more soft spoken and calculated with his words. "That boy enjoys being around his family and has the greatest one-liners. Those four are a close-knit bunch. I am so thankful for their relationships with one another."

Sarah helped Mary with setting the table while listening to her carry on about her family.

"God knew what He was doing giving us Billy first. He's an excellent role model, always so encouraging and positive. My only complaint is that we don't get to see him often enough. I guess I could say that about all my kids. Even Frankie, who still lives at home, is busy every night of the week. I have learned to soak up the moments when everyone is together, relaxing at home."

Sarah replied, "Your family sounds a lot like mine. I have older siblings who have shaped and guided me along with my parents. How does the famous saying go… it takes a village? It's been nice to hear about your family and see your glow when you speak of them. Who knows, maybe someday, I'll get to meet them in person." Sarah smirked and shrugged before sitting down at the table.

Mary joined her. "Well, if the weather doesn't cooperate in Missouri, you may actually end up getting to meet the guys sooner than later."

CHAPTER 10

"This place is so beautiful!" Sarah said to the unfamiliar man. They were walking hand in hand on the gorgeous beach in Turks and Caicos.

"Thank you for inviting me to come along with you on your work trip, Sarah! I just wish we were getting married on the beach rather than those people," the man said pointing to the small, intimate wedding happening at the moment. "I'm not sure there is a more perfect setting than sunset at Grace Bay Beach." He turned to Sarah and kissed her with a passion so deep, she felt it all the way to her toes.

"I want nothing more than to marry you someday, but it's just not the right time. I still have to figure out what I want to be when I grow up. I feel I'm getting closer. I'm not sure why that is, but I have a strong feeling that I will understand it soon. This doesn't seem fair to ask you this, but, please, can you wait for me to figure this out?" Sarah pleaded while looking into the man's mesmerizing eyes.

"You are the most amazing woman I've ever met, Sarah! We were sent to each other in the most unpredictable way. I'm pretty sure I would be testing fate by walking away from you. Plus, I couldn't walk away if I tried. You have me hooked!"

And with that he faded away.

"Wait, wait, don't go!" Sarah whimpers. "Wait! Please stay!"

Sarah stared at the ceiling, trying to decipher between her dream and reality. Her heart felt a heaviness from the man fading away. Then she smiled at herself, realizing it was a dream. Her thoughts pondered the meaning behind her dream and that mystery man.

"Who was that guy?" she asked herself as she sat still a few moments longer until the smell of coffee wafting up from the kitchen motivated her to get out of bed.

Sarah readied herself to go downstairs when her phone buzzed. *Do I even want to check that message?* she wondered as she walked back to the bedside table to fetch her phone.

"Ugh I knew it! Why did I even check?" Sarah rolled her eyes and sighed with submission. Then she tossed her phone onto the bed and walked downstairs.

"Good morning, Mary!" Sarah walked into the familiar kitchen and fetched herself a coffee mug. "How'd the house fair last night after the storms?"

Mary was sitting at the island with her warm mug between her hands. "Good morning to you as well, Sarah! Things are looking a little rough outside right now. I walked Tito earlier this morning between rain showers and noticed two big trees down blocking the lake road."

Mary looked down at her coffee somberly.

"I feel horrible, Sarah, but I'm not sure how you will make your flight when we have one tree still down in the driveway and now some across the road as well." Mary sighed. "I have a call in to our tree guy, but unfortunately, he won't make it to our house if he can't get down the street. I don't even know who to call about those trees because they are near power lines."

Sarah, with a softened look, approached Mary. "Please don't worry about it. My damn flight was delayed again. I was rebooked on the 7:00 p.m. flight." Pointing to the TV, Sarah said, "And who knows if that will even happen. It looks like we might be in for another round of unpredictable storms today."

Refilling her mug, Mary explained with disbelief, "For as long as I can remember, we haven't had quite so many consistent pop-up storms like this. I'm worried my boys will have to end their hunt early because of saturated fields in Missouri." Mary frowned slightly. "It would be a shame for them to lose their time together. It's the one time my husband can truly dial down and just enjoy being with the boys."

The coffee mug suddenly felt heavy in Sarah's hands, and she had to sit down. "I'm beginning to think I've brought a cloud of bad luck with me. So much has happened since I arrived on Saturday." She avoided Mary's glance but then brushed a strand of hair away and looked up. "Could you imagine if I was stuck alone in that cottage with weather like this? Mary, I definitely think you are my guardian angel. I don't know what I would've done without you."

Mary replied, "Thank you, Sarah! You have been an angel for me too. I would've been quite nervous being alone last night when the power went out. As unique as our meeting was, it was all part of God's plan."

After sitting for a few moments in silence, watching the weather report on TV, Mary looked at Sarah with a warm smile.

"Sarah, what would you think of staying here for the rest of the week? It would be reassuring to have someone else around with this unpredictable weather. Plus, you could get your writing done as you'd originally planned."

Without much hesitation Sarah looked at Mary and smiled. "It seems my planning efforts continue to be flipped upside down. Maybe it would be best to loosen my grip and be good with what's in front of me. If you really mean it, I will take you up on it." Sarah surprised herself with how quickly the words of acceptance rolled from her mouth.

Mary gently put her hand on Sarah's arm. "It would be my pleasure to have you stay here and a delight to know that a soon-to-be-published author put the finishing touches on her manuscript at my home."

Sarah laughed. "I think we both have some work to get done. Selfishly, I want to read a new Mary Katherine Thomas novel soon, so I almost want you to write more than I want to myself."

Sarah had only done about three hours of solid edits since leaving Boston. She knew this familiar nagging feeling stirring inside of her. She needed to focus and get to work. Yet she also needed some exercise, or at least fresh air to get the creative juices flowing. Slurping down her last sips of coffee, she asked Mary, "It looks like we have a little break before the next round of storms. I think I might go for a run but don't want to veer too far in case storms come faster than predicted. Is there a trail you'd suggest?"

Mary perked up with Sarah's request. "Great idea! Exercise will help the brain. As for a trail, it all depends how far you want to go. Often times I just go around the lake, which is almost exactly four miles. If you get started soon, you should have time to fit that in."

Sarah put on her headphones and headed out for her run around the little lake she had become so fond of. The storm had left the neighborhood quite a mess. The downed trees and branches formed obstacles for her as she exited the lake road, which led her thoughts to drift to the many obstacles she had encountered in her young life. It seemed her occasional pivots, in plans and decisions, ended up being blessings in disguise. *If only I could live life backward, I wouldn't have wasted so much time obsessing over the things I couldn't control.*

Sarah's music triggered a memory from college. It was playing at the restaurant the night she met Cory. *He was so hot!* She thought back to that first encounter when she noticed his blond hair flopping out the back of his baseball hat. Sarah smiled as she rounded the south end of the lake predicting she had to be around mile one of four. The west sky was getting dark again, yet she was lost in her memory of Cory.

* * *

It was a perfect fall day. Sarah was sitting outside at a Mexican restaurant with her best friend, Jo. Sipping on margaritas, excited they didn't get IDed, they were in their own world when two very cute guys approached their table and asked to join them.

Cory immediately drew Sarah in with his deep-set, hazel eyes. His vision locked on hers as if they were the only two people outside that restaurant. "Hi there. Sarah, is it?"

Sarah had definitely noticed Cory from parties and other events on campus. She wanted to chat with him many times but didn't have the courage.

Sarah answered, trying to keep her composure by downplaying her response, "Hi, how are you? Do I know you from somewhere?"

"I'm Cory, and this is my buddy, Grant. We haven't officially met, but I've seen you around. It looks like you two are having fun. Mind if we join you?"

Sarah and Jo looked at each other and said at the same time, "No problem!"

"Great!" The guys pulled out chairs, placing them closer to the girls than each other.

The four proceeded to have fun for another few hours before they decided it was time to change scenery. Though Sarah and Jo were underage, Cory and Grant were legal and knew the bouncer at the hot spot for college kids.

"This is our lucky night!" Jo said looking back at Sarah, holding Grant's hand as they walked past the bouncer.

Cory leaned down and whispered in Sarah's ear, "I gotta be honest about something!"

She looked worried. "Oh no, do you have a girlfriend? Seriously, I don't need some girl pissed off at me for hanging out with you."

Cory put his hands on her arms to calm her down. "No, no, there's not a girlfriend. What I wanted to tell you was that I knew exactly who you were when Grant and I saw you at the restaurant. I first noticed you in the humanities building last year because our classes got done at the same time. Then I saw you at a few parties and asked my friends if they knew you."

"Wait! What? You've been asking about me?" With wide eyes, she pointed to herself.

Sarah, in disbelief at what she was hearing, smiled as Cory continued, "Something about you, Sarah, just caught my eye. Every time I saw you, you were having a great time, just like tonight! Your smile lights up your whole face!"

Sarah was in awe but tried to play it cool now wondering if this guy was just a player. "I'm not sure what I should say to all of that. Should I be worried you're a stalker?" She smirked at him, and they both laughed.

That night led to a lighthearted and brief relationship, which was just what Sarah needed to get her mind off of

Henry for a while. Her feelings for Cory were strong but more like a crush. At that time, she didn't have the strength to pursue another long-term relationship, especially when still confused about where she wanted things to go with her own life, much less future plans with Henry.

* * *

Sarah's pace was picking up with the light rain setting in. She thought she maybe had another mile to go before getting back to Mary's. Her mind drifted back to Cory. She still got butterflies in her stomach when she thought of the night they officially met. He was a great guy, and the time with him proved that she was not closed off to love after Henry. The relationship was a fun one at the beginning but then became too intense too fast. Cory started to get clingy as she spoke more about leaving to study abroad, and he was showing signs of jealousy when she'd talk to other guys. It didn't take long for the lighthearted fun to be replaced by the "ick" feeling in her gut.

Hindsight offered a clear perspective. It was a blessing that he ended up giving her the "icks." She knew her sense of loyalty well enough, and she would've stayed back for the sake of keeping the relationship going. The semester she studied abroad opened up the window of opportunity to see places in the world she had only seen in pictures. Her love of travel was broadened, and her blogs about her experiences brought her into the job she had now. The famous saying, "All things happen for a reason," popped into her head at that moment. Looking back, she could finally agree with that statement.

CHAPTER 11

Sarah arrived back at the house just as thunder started to rumble. As always, the physical activity invigorated her, and the brain dump, as she referred to it, provided clarity. "Hi, Mary, I'm back!" Sarah said walking in the front door. She heard the faint sound of keyboard clicking from Mary's office.

"Hey, Sarah! I'm just adding a few more snippets for my book."

Sarah stood in the doorway of Mary's office. "You keep on your roll. I had a few ideas during my run, so I'm going to head upstairs and start writing as well."

Mary's hands rested on her keyboard while she looked up. "Sounds like you had a productive time out. The radar looks like the Midwest will be seeing more storms and high winds throughout the day. Hopefully no tornados. Plan for it to be a good writing day."

The morning had quickly shifted to the late afternoon when Sarah realized she hadn't looked up from her computer in almost four hours. She had found Elizabeth's room with its white painted trim and subtle grey walls to be quite the inspiring writer's haven. *This room is way better than the dingy cottage would've been,* Sarah thought while she pushed her chair away from the desk to stand up and stretch.

Now looking out the window, she noticed there was something floating or bobbing in the water near the end of the pier.

Is that a big tree branch? she wondered as she squinted to get a better look. *Wait, no, those are the yellow Adirondack chairs.* She remembered seeing them when she arrived. Enjoying the excuse to step away from her computer for a bit, she went downstairs to tell Mary about the chairs.

"Thanks for reminding me. I noticed those earlier but was waiting for the rain to pass. It's very shallow out there, so that obviously helped to keep the chairs from drifting off and sinking during the crazy weather." Mary walked over to the window closest to the lake and said, "Well, looks like this might be the break in rain I was waiting for. This may be the only opportunity all day to get them out."

Sarah asked if she could help, and within minutes the two ladies changed into shorts and were on the pier strategizing the best approach.

With the high wind swirling around them, they had to raise their voices to hear each other. Mary yelled while her long blonde hair blew in front of her face, "Looks like the storms lodged the chairs into the mucky bottom. We can give it a try, but it might be more than either of us want to deal with right now. What do you think? You up for it?"

Sarah yelled back, "We got this!" while she hopped into the thigh-high shallow water. She squealed loudly. "Holy shit, it's cold!" Sarah giggled and walked toward the bobbing chairs while waves splashed her face.

"I like your style, Sarah!" Mary said as she jumped in right behind her. "Holy crap! You weren't kidding. Damn, it's cold!" The two women worked together getting the first heavy chair onto the pier and decided to carry it safely to shore so it wouldn't blow in again.

As they set the first chair down, Mary, now tying her windblown hair back with a hair scrunchie, said, "Thanks so much for helping me. I definitely would've blown right into the water carrying that bad boy to shore on my own."

They walked back to the pier to fetch the second chair when a gust of wind blew Sarah right into Mary. "Ahhh!" They screamed at the same time followed by a laugh. "Yep, you definitely would've blown in the water with that gust, Mary. Nothing like a little wind resistance training."

The second chair was sunken deeper into the sand than the first one, so Mary suggested they leave it until the next day when the heavy winds subsided.

"Are you sure?" Sarah asked. "I don't mind trying to muscle this one."

Mary pointed to the west, over the house, and said, "Based on the scary-looking clouds, I think it's best we wait on this chair." No sooner did Mary finish speaking than a loud crack of thunder had the ladies right out of the water and racing for shelter in the house.

Thunder continued, and lightning wasn't too far behind it. The storm brought night time darkness a little sooner than normal while the two women settled into their familiar placements in the kitchen. Sarah sat at the end of the island, and Mary leaned against it. They chatted about their individual writing progress from the day and laughed more at the funny happenings during the chair rescue.

"I'm not sure how I'd weather any of these storms without your company, Sarah," Mary said. "Based on the past two days, I think we both have some good material for our next books. Shit, maybe we could combine our stories and write a book together."

Sarah looked at Mary with wide eyes and responded with a high pitch thrill, "Are you kidding me? That would be a dream come true! Can we start now?"

Mary blushed. "I love your confidence, Sarah!" Mary's attention was redirected from Sarah when her phone started ringing. "Let's table that topic for a moment. It looks like Frank is calling," Mary said while picking up her phone and walking down the hall toward her office.

Sarah found herself getting lost in thought about her future. *What if this author gig becomes my next career move? What if Mary and I actually brought this daydream to reality? We could write a fictional story about how we met. The serendipitous nature of it would keep readers engaged yet enlightened.*

Sarah thought about the timing of this trip and how, up until a week ago, she wasn't even planning to leave Boston to work on her final edits. Now she was staying in the house of a famous author, daydreaming about writing a book together. Talk about divine intervention. At this moment, Sarah was washed over with an immense sense of gratitude. She looked up and said, "Thank you, God!"

With a smile on her face, Sarah continued to reflect on what their book cover could look like. Would it have a picture of the tranquil lake, or maybe a stormy look with the floating yellow Adirondack chairs?

"This could be fun!" she said while nodding.

Sarah heard the ping of her phone and looked to see a text from Henry. And just like that, the previous happy thought was quickly invaded by a heavier one. The image of Henry once again popped into her mind.

Sarah remembered the conversation she and Mary had on the first night, still strangers at the time, regarding perfect timing and discovering purpose. She thought about Henry and wondered if she made a mistake by not getting back together with him when he returned from Notre Dame. This same thought reoccurred more often than she cared to admit. *Why can I not let it go?* she wondered.

Although Sarah knew, in her heart, she did the right thing by allowing herself independence and personal space in college, she couldn't figure out why her thoughts drifted back to Henry now and again. She flashed back to earlier times and one of many conversations about their future.

* * *

Sarah ended up dating Henry, who was her best friend at the time, for the last two years of high school through freshmen year of college. During that time, they had numerous hypothetical conversations about their future. Would they go to college, and where? Would they get married young and have kids right away like their parents did? Or would they work and travel for a while before kids? Sarah loved to travel and had a strong desire to see new places. Henry did not!

Henry loved his hometown, spending time with his parents and older sister. He enjoyed the security of his friends and teammates. He played lacrosse in high school and earned a scholarship at Notre Dame. Henry was a good guy with simple ideals. He had his life planned out. Sarah, on the other hand, was still working to put the pieces of the puzzle together.

Sarah remembered Henry clearly saying to her when he was about to leave for freshmen year, "Sarah, after college, I want to work as a financial planner, like my dad. He has a sweet setup for me right after graduation. I won't have any stress with finding a job."

Sarah was shocked by the unwavering certainty in his voice.

Henry continued, "It will be perfect. We'll get married and have kids right away, just like our parents. You'll get to stay home with the kids, and I'll work. Doesn't that sound great?" Henry asked her with a genuine glowing smile. Sarah smiled back at him because she thought she wanted those things as well. She was so in love with Henry. Therefore, all she really wanted was to be with him, even if it meant molding her dreams into his.

* * *

Sarah faintly heard Mary talking to her and snapped back into reality. "Well it sounds like the second half of the hunting trip has not gone as planned."

Sarah turned her head. "Oh no, what's going on?"

Mary opened her mouth to reply when her phone rang again. "I'm sorry, Sarah, it's Frank again. We got disconnected before. I won't be long," she said as she walked back toward her office.

Sarah continued thinking of how she and Henry broke up after freshmen year and from that point on never officially got back together. They would see each other periodically when home from school for holiday breaks, which repeatedly led to bouts of texting or calling for weeks afterward. Often, Henry would call Sarah after being out at night. He would end every call with a flirty comment and talk about their future. He was relentless with his plan to get her back.

Sarah, on the other hand, never returned the gesture of calling late at night. Throughout their final years of college, she reached out via text a couple times to check-in, but mostly Henry had initiated their conversations.

Not sure what to expect, Sarah picked up her phone to read Henry's text.

Henry: *How are you, Sarah? Are you still on your little writer's retreat?*

Henry often belittled her career as well as her love for writing. Sarah, frustrated, sighed and, beyond her better judgment, kept reading his text.

Henry: *I am heading your way for a one-day financial meeting with regional planners and wondered if maybe you'd like to grab dinner?*

Pondering how to respond, Sarah put down her phone and walked the four steps to the open wine bottle sitting on the kitchen counter.

CHAPTER 12

Sarah looked up while she refilled her glass to see Mary set her phone down across the island from her. "So what's the word from Frank? Are they able to hunt tomorrow?"

Mary replied confidently, "I can guarantee if it's possible for those boys to hunt, they will. Although Frank did sound pretty disappointed on the phone."

The kitchen was quiet other than a baseball game playing on the TV in the background. A new heaviness sat in the room. Sarah could tell Mary was affected by her husband's disappointment and wondered what it would be like to feel so deeply for another person. *Is Henry my only shot at lasting love?* she wondered. She questioned if maybe she needed to open her heart and mind again to this idea yet knew he was engaged. *That ship has obviously sailed,* Sarah reminded herself. *Or has it?* She questioned. And with that thought she excused herself from the kitchen. "Mary, I'll be right back to help with dinner. I just need to run upstairs to make a phone call."

Mary, looking into the fridge, said, "No rush, Sarah. I'll put out a smorgasbord of items to pick at for dinner." Mary laughed. "Take your time!"

Henry was quick to pick up after two rings. "Hi, Sarah, perfect timing. I was just looking at my phone to see if you replied to the earlier text. How are you?"

Sarah replied, "Hi, Henry. I'm well. I'm still working on finalizing my book." Sarah took a deep breath, remembering the comment he made about her little writer's retreat. "Honestly, I'm quite excited about my progress. This trip has served me well so far."

Henry skimmed briefly over her comment and proceeded, "That's nice, Sarah. So what do you think about grabbing dinner on Wednesday night? I know it's only two days away, but I assumed you weren't too busy and maybe would enjoy a good meal on me."

Frustrated with his disregard, Sarah felt foolish for her earlier thoughts of lasting love. She rolled her eyes and wondered why she considered having dinner with him at all. "Okay, Henry. I'll meet you there, just text me the name of the restaurant."

Henry, always wanting to be in control, said, "How about I pick you up? Please send me the address of where you're staying."

Sarah finished the brief call. "Sounds good. Let me know if something changes. It's not a problem to just meet you."

Sarah haphazardly tossed her phone on Elizabeth's bed before heading downstairs to enjoy the time with her idol. As she approached the landing, she could see Mary preparing some sort of concoction. "Is there anything I can do? I have barely helped at all."

Mary placed some croutons onto the island next to what looked like salad fixings. "Not to worry. It's not like I've been making the fanciest meals." Mary chuckled. "On a different note, when I took Tito on a walk earlier, I noticed some neighbors using their UTVs to pull trees from the middle of the road. Seemed easy enough. Since my tree guy is in high demand from all the storm damage, I'm thinking I might ask those neighbors to help me move the tree to the side of the driveway. At least we'd be able to get our cars out. Thank God for great neighbors!"

Sarah nodded in agreement. "No kidding! People aren't always so lucky to have helpful neighbors like that. Although the verdict is still out on the neighbor who owns the lot with the missing cottage."

Setting the table with two dinner places, Mary inquired, "Speaking of that, did you ever get to the bottom of what happened with your rental property?"

Sarah rolled her eyes and slapped her forehead slightly saying, "Oh my gosh, to be honest Mary, I completely forgot to do more digging on that. I called the credit card company and informed them I was scammed, but I forgot to investigate further. I'll have to do that tomorrow. I can't believe how this day has gotten away from me. I'm so thankful for the writing I was able to get done earlier."

The two women sat at the table for an hour chatting over their Caesar salads and cheesecake.

Sarah brought up their earlier conversation, "So Mary, about the co-authoring idea we chatted about earlier. I think that is a magnificent idea, and I'd be over-the-moon excited about my name being next to yours on a book cover. Oh my gosh, we could go on book tours together! We could hit the road and have some fun!"

Mary paused to absorb Sarah's enthusiasm and offered, "Truthfully, Sarah, that may be just the kick in the ass I need to give my writing a purpose. Currently I just keep a running document of snippets that may someday make up a book, but I haven't actually started with a story line yet." Mary mentioned her doubts about finishing another book on her own with the various yet welcomed distractions from family as well as volunteer obligations. "Frank and the kids are strongly encouraging me to write another book, yet I remember all too well the time commitment involved in the writing and publishing process."

Mary took a deep breath and finished her remaining wine.

"When I was younger, my motivation to finish my books was purely professional, but now it would be more of a personal goal. It would be so rewarding for my kids to see me as an author again rather than only a mom. For that reason, if I actually start a book, I will carry it through until the finished product." Mary smiled sweetly while she stood up from the table and carried her dishes to the sink. She continued, "And the idea of co-authoring a book with you would definitely make the process more fun!"

Sarah wasn't far behind her with her own dishes. "It would be a blast! And we already have a story line rolling out before our eyes with all that's happened in the short time we've known each other."

The two laughed.

After washing and drying the few dishes they used, Sarah asked, "Don't you think it's interesting timing, and a bit serendipitous, that we met at these exact stages in our lives? You stepping back into the author world and me beginning as a newbie." She put her palms together in a prayer gesture. "God has to be smiling down on us and probably smirking, too, because he knows the ultimate plan. We just need to be patient and wait for it to unfold for us."

The ladies, done with the dinner cleanup, moved their conversation to the sunroom. Sarah took a seat on the sectional couch, resting her feet on the foot stool, while Mary sat in Frank's chair.

Mary said, "Well, it sounds like you and I may have some brainstorming to do. I know Frank would be damn excited for me if I followed through with another book."

Sarah added, "I hope I get to meet Frank someday. He sounds like quite an amazing husband and so supportive of you."

Mary nodded in agreement. "He really is awesome! I need to tell him that more often."

Sarah, looking down at her wine glass, pondered Mary's words briefly and then said, "I can only pray I find an awesome man like Frank. Who knows, maybe my 'Frank' is closer than I think and I just need to be less guarded. I wouldn't doubt it if my family has bets on how long it will take for me to be married to someone other than my work." Sarah laughed out loud of that idea.

Mary smiled yet had a look of confusion in her eyes as she asked Sarah politely what her age was.

Sarah responded, "I'm already twenty-seven."

Quick to the reply, Mary said, "You mean you're *only* twenty-seven? You are a bright young woman with a lifetime ahead of you. You look so young, yet the way you've been talking I thought there was pressure of a biological time clock ticking. I hope you don't mind me offering you a reframe on your age perspective, but the way I see it, you have plenty of time to find your perfect companion. Therefore, right now should be time to focus on you. Soak up the independence of making decisions just for you. Who knows, the next guy you date could be the last guy you date."

They looked at each other and smiled. Sarah thanked Mary for her perspective change. "I like your thought process, Mary. And helping to instill a sense of hope."

Mary let Tito out and turned to Sarah. "And maybe that boy from home you talked about the other night will end up being the one for you after all."

Sarah smirked. "Ironic you should bring up Henry. I was on the phone with him earlier, and it sounds like he'll be in town on Wednesday for some work meetings. Their family owns a financial planning franchise with associates working all over the country. From what Henry said, he has reps working in this area as well. Who would've thought?" Sarah shrugged her shoulders. "He asked if I wanted to get dinner. It will be nice to see him. There won't, however, be any future other than friends. He's engaged to a sweet girl from our hometown."

Mary let Tito back inside. "It's nice you could preserve a friendship. That often isn't the case after those long-term relationships."

Sarah concluded by saying, "It's definitely not as clear-cut as I make it sound. In fact, things have gotten murky, especially since college ended, but that may be a story for a different day."

Mary yawned. "We can continue this tomorrow over coffee. I so wish Elizabeth was here. She would love these conversations, and I have a feeling you two would hit it off great!"

Sarah could see a little sadness in Mary's eyes and knew she was missing her daughter. She empathized. "I hope I get to meet her someday. And rest assured that Elizabeth is growing in leaps and bounds with her abroad experience. She will have a ton of stories to share with you when she returns. I remember it felt like it took weeks to fill my mom in on everything when I returned from Italy."

Mary perked up. "Thank you! I look forward to hearing more about your experiences overseas. It will help give me perspective on what Elizabeth is experiencing now." Mary yawned again. "But I think it's time I hit the hay. Let's chat more tomorrow."

CHAPTER 13

Sarah suddenly realized the man of her dreams was lowering himself to one knee. He looked up at her, his face blurry except for his captivating eyes as he said...

Sarah startled awake. "Not again!" she said with lighthearted frustration. "Why do I keep waking up just when the dream gets good?"

Sarah was taken aback by the sight of the sun twinkling off the lake. *A girl could easily get used to this place!* she thought with a cheerful vibe. *It's going to be a great day! I can feel it.*

Without brushing her hair or teeth, still in her pajama pants and old Boston University T-shirt, Sarah stumbled downstairs to retrieve a cup of coffee and bring it back to Elizabeth's room. She planned to get an hour of editing in before heading out. While pouring her coffee, she heard Mary coming in the front door talking to someone. *Must be the tree guy,* Sarah thought while she walked to the fridge to grab creamer.

"Good morning, Sarah!" she heard Mary say. While holding the creamer bottle in her hand and wedging the fridge open with her elbow, Sarah slowly looked over her right shoulder to say hi to Mary and noticed it wasn't just Mary. Four men were walking into the kitchen with her. Sarah, now fully aware of what she must look like, was blushing in embarrassment.

"Sarah, I'd like to introduce you to my husband, Frank, and my boys, Billy, Scotty, and Frankie. It was quite the surprise to see them walking in the door this morning when I came out of my bedroom."

Sarah closed the fridge and turned to look at the crew gathered around. Though she was embarrassed, she wasn't going to let them notice that. Sarah held her mug with one hand while making a waving gesture. "Hi, gentlemen! I'm Sarah. Nice to meet you."

Almost in unison the guys said hello to the strange woman standing in their kitchen. As the men went about the room, Mary proceeded to fill Sarah in on the story. "Frank texted me last night, but I fell asleep before seeing it. He said they were going to drive home during the night. Apparently the last two days of the hunt were canceled due to flooding in the fields and more rain expected yet this week. I walked out of the bedroom to call our tree guy just as they were walking in the front door. It was a terrific surprise for me, but I don't think the guys are too happy about being back so early." Mary pointed to them outside the front window as they unloaded their stuff from the truck. "The boys were able to drag the tree to the side of the driveway so they could pull the truck closer to the house. Now we can finally get out too!"

Sarah looked out the window to see the guys with slumped posture as they unpacked their belongings. "That's great news about the tree, but I feel so bad for them that their trip was disrupted." Sarah looked back at Mary standing a few feet beyond her. "Can I do anything to help? I feel a little strange being in your home now that it's a full house."

"Don't be silly! You are a welcomed guest in our house, and I'm thankful you were with me this weekend. Please carry on as you planned. I'm pretty sure the guys will head to bed for a couple of hours this morning. It sounds like they were all awake for most of the drive home from Missouri," Mary reassured her.

Sarah walked toward the stairs with her steaming coffee. "Well now that the driveway is clear I think I'll plan to make a run to the market and refill your food stash."

Mary chuckled. "Sweet of you to offer but please don't even think about it, my dear! With the hearty appetites back in the house, I will need to triple my grocery list. I'm thinking a homemade lasagna would appease for dinner tonight."

"That sounds great! I have a wonderful family recipe for lasagna! Would you let me make dinner for you all?" Sarah offered while peeking her head over the banister.

Mary stood in the front foyer and looked up at Sarah, giving her a double thumbs up. "Deal! Please let me know what ingredients you'd like me to pick up. I will head to the store in about an hour once things settle down with this troop." Mary pointed outside at her boys who were almost done emptying their truck. Mary looked upstairs again. "And, Sarah, I meant it when I said you should continue with your week as planned. Even though we'll have more activity than originally planned, nobody will bother you. I imagine that tomorrow Frank will most likely go into the office, Billy will head back to Chicago, and Scotty and Frankie will go to their respective schools."

Sarah walked back down a few stairs to be closer to Mary. "I appreciate this so much. This all feels like a dream to me, and one I will continue to enjoy."

Sarah enjoyed her coffee in Elizabeth's room, looking over the lake. She thought about the conversation she'd had with Henry last night and wondered if she was setting herself up for more frustration by agreeing to meet him for dinner. They'd not seen each other in years, ever since she'd dropped off the key to his apartment.

And what about Erin? Surely, Henry had told her that we were meeting. Right? Either way, that was between the two of them. Sarah needed to focus today. Energized from caffeine and sunshine, she was looking forward to a productive day.

Sarah was efficient with her hour of work. She chipped away at her final edits and felt it was a good time to get outside.

Dressed for her run, she sat down on the steps to tie her shoes. She looked up as one of Mary's sons walked toward her. She couldn't help but notice the kindness around his amazing blue eyes. Sarah was taken aback.

"So you're Sarah! Nice to meet you in person. I'm Billy." Billy reached out to shake her hand. "I need to apologize for being rude on the phone the other night."

Sarah stood up and was immediately mesmerized. She shook his hand in slow motion, as if hypnotized. "No problem at all. I completely understand." And then realizing what she was doing, she added, "Oh, my gosh, I am so sorry. You probably think I'm a weirdo. You just look so familiar." Sarah snapped out of her trance-like state, now speaking nervously. "Have you ever been to the Boston area? Why do you look so familiar? These kinds of things bother me until I figure them out."

Billy leaned against the back of the sofa with his hands in his front pockets and looked down at Sarah still sitting on the steps. "I've been to Boston with my family on a couple of vacations. Did my mom mention that her brother lives west of the city? Also, her best friend lives north of Boston. What a beautiful area!"

Sarah picked up her empty mug from the stairs, and Billy walked alongside her the few steps to the kitchen. "It seems your mom and I talked almost nonstop since she invited me to stay here on Saturday, but she never mentioned it. I'll have to ask her more about it later on. I'm happy you liked the city. I went to college at BU and then stayed in the city after I graduated. It hasn't gotten old to me yet." Sarah rinsed her mug and turned to Billy, who plopped on the stool closest to the sink. "Your mom did mention you live in Chicago now. That's a great city as well! I've only been there a few times but had a blast every time!"

Billy was slightly slouched with arms resting on the island. "Thanks. I like it too!" He sighed. "Good for you to be heading out for a run. Thinking my workout will have to wait until after I get some sleep. Nice to meet you. Have a good run!"

Sarah offered a flirtatious smile. "Thanks, Billy! Nice to meet you too. Sleep well."

Sarah subtly watched Billy meander out of the kitchen and head upstairs. At that moment, Mary and Frank walked in the front door. "Looks like you're ready for a run," Frank said.

Then Mary interrupted, "At least you don't have to dodge raindrops today." They both laughed, remembering Sarah's rainy run the other day. Mary had a bigger smile than Sarah had yet to see.

"Thank you! Maybe I'll make it a little longer run today. And, Frank, it's nice that I was able to meet you and your boys. I'm sorry your trip was shortened, but I certainly can see it makes Mary happy to have you all home. Well, here I go! Hopefully I don't get lost." Sarah smirked while putting her earphones in and took off down the driveway.

She was still smiling even when she passed the open lot that was supposed to be her rental cottage. *Such a surreal turn of events. Meeting Mary has been a true gift from God. There is no other way to look at it!* She pointed to the heavens and mouthed, "Thank you!"

Per usual the road was Sarah's release and re-energizer, yet today she didn't need either. She felt light on her feet, almost as if she was floating with each step. *I wish I could bottle this feeling!* she thought, already clipping off mile one. Sarah remembered back to one of her work trips when she enjoyed a similar floating sensation while out for a run.

* * *

She was at one of her favorite locations for work and out for a morning run on the hilly and very treacherous roads in St. John. She remembered feeling like she was gliding along the road, with the warm sun on her face and just a hint of needed breeze at her back. It was December, so the sun felt extra warm compared to the cold winter she'd been experiencing in Boston.

Sarah was traveling solo, like most trips, yet she never seemed to mind. She took a liking to being in control of her own schedule and loved being able to write as long as needed without distractions. The unfortunate downfall of this trip was its shorter-than-normal duration. She was staying for two nights and then heading home just in time for the holidays. The original itinerary had her visit scheduled after the holidays and staying longer, but her boss wanted the article done before the new year. He wanted the article to focus on the island in the heart of winter when people were looking for a quick and easy escape. *St. John was definitely an escape,* Sarah thought. She'd been all around the world, yet for some reason, this place felt magical. She could've sworn the blue water actually sparkled like diamonds last night. *What's more magical than sparkling water at night?* She was running down the long driveway to her resort. "Breakfast is calling my name," she said.

The waitress directed her to a spot that once again allowed for the warm sun to hit her face. She closed her eyes and took a deep breath, feeling a sense of calm wash over her. *The perks of the job,* she thought. And a job she already loved, so the perks were just a bonus.

Sarah smiled as the adorable waitress poured coffee and asked about her morning. "You look like you were exercising. Not many do that on vacation, so kudos to you!"

Sarah filled her in that she was there for work and asked for her name. She continued the conversation, asking the waitress if she would mind answering some questions for her next article.

"Sure, I'm happy to answer questions, but do I have to have my name mentioned?" The waitress smiled.

"Not at all. I will note you as an anonymous source."

Sarah enjoyed breakfast while catching up on social media. She scrolled through the many photos of people with their kids and dogs when she noticed a post by Henry. *He never posts,* she mused as she clicked on the photos that must've been from an awards function for work.

Sarah thought about the last time she saw him, which was just a couple days prior to that trip. He waved her over to chat when he was out for coffee with a client. She remembered how he questioned why she'd want to work for someone who sent her away so close to the holidays. "It's not a problem. I'll be back in time for the festivities," she mentioned to him and then walked away. *Why did he even care?*

Sarah stared at the twinkly blue water thinking about Henry and his need to feel superior. He wasn't like that when they were younger. Or maybe he was and she just didn't notice. She noticed her pleasant mood had shifted downward when a voice coming from the TV behind her spoke about an unexpected winter storm heading toward the East Coast of the United States. She got up from her chair and walked closer to the bar area where the TV hung on the wall so she could hear the broadcaster better.

"Airports are bracing for a messy Christmas with the latest forecast of up to a foot of snow along the upper East Coast," the broadcaster continued.

"Oh no! What crappy timing. I need to get home now!" Sarah's shoulders slouched, and with the depressing news, she went back to her table to change her flight, which was currently scheduled to leave the following afternoon, two days before Christmas. She needed to get on the afternoon flight today, but no seats were left and no other flights were going home today. Her terrific mood was now ruined at the idea she would be stuck there and miss being home for Christmas Eve mass and traditional festivities that followed. Sarah was beyond upset yet knew from similar travel issues that occurred in the past that it was best to stay calm. She booked herself on the Christmas flight in hopes that the storm scheduled for the following night would be cleaned up by then.

For being only twenty-five, Sarah had almost a full passport. She had been in this dream job for a little over a year and couldn't imagine working anywhere else, but for the first time, she was upset with the timing of her placement. She knew she had to call her mom and tell her she would not be there for Christmas Eve. *Ugh, this is going to break her heart and mine,* Sarah thought as a tear rolled down her face.

That sadness was quickly replaced with a brief moment of anger. *Wait until she runs into Henry at mass and tells him I'm stuck on assignment. I can see his smug face already has if he won an imaginary argument.* And she knew exactly what he would say to her mom, "I told her she shouldn't work. If she'd stayed with me, she'd be home for Christmas not stuck on some island."

* * *

Sarah's mind snapped back to the present moment with a sense of frustration. Her pace grew quicker as she transferred her anger to the road beneath her feet. *Why did I allow myself to worry about what he thought?* she questioned herself.

Sarah tried to replace the negative thoughts with the pleasantness she felt earlier in her run. Though she was upset with her boss for sending her away so close to Christmas, she reframed her thoughts to accept her situation for what it was. She remembered how the sadness on that particular trip to St. John was replaced with that magical island feeling. Natural beauty and wonderful people surrounded her. The restaurant put together an amazing Christmas Eve meal, and her sweet waitress gave her extra special attention that night so she didn't feel alone.

Sarah's mom called her back to say she wouldn't miss a thing because all Christmas Eve celebrations would be shifting to Christmas night due to bad weather. Sarah smiled as she remembered the feeling of walking into her parents' home Christmas night and being greeted with a million hugs and kisses. *There, that's what I needed to bring me back to happy again!* St. John and Christmas night ended up being the most blessed stretch of days. Again, God is in the details. She walked up Mary's driveway.

Sarah walked into the noiseless house and felt immediately at home. Crazy how a few days could make such a difference in someone's life. She quietly went back to Elizabeth's room for a shower and an afternoon of editing.

CHAPTER 14

Looking outside, Sarah could see the sunniness of earlier being replaced with a mysterious gray sky.

"Mary, do you know if it's supposed to storm tonight? The sky has that ominous, calm-before-the-storm look to it."

Mary replied, "Possibly some rain, but nothing that looked worrisome. I think we've had enough storms this week! Any more and we might need to build ourselves an ark." They both laughed while Mary finished setting the table.

Sarah wore one of Mary's aprons and looked like an experienced chef. "This will be fun! Thanks for letting me cook for you and the guys tonight." Sarah had the ingredients organized on the island and then walked around the kitchen, opening doors and drawers until she found the utensils and pans she needed.

Mary ventured to the wet bar to retrieve some wine and then handed a glass to Sarah. "I have to admit, there is a sense of peace knowing the house is full, but all is quiet. My heart is almost as content as it gets. I just need Elizabeth home, too, and all would be perfect in my little world."

Sarah looked up to notice Mary's calm look. Not sad, yet not bursting with happiness either. Somewhere in the middle. "That reminds me of something my mom would say. I do get that. When I was little, nothing was better in my world than when all of my siblings were home at the same time. That didn't happen too often, but when it did, I wanted the world to stop. I can't even imagine how it must feel as a mom of grown children when the chickens are in the nest."

Mary smiled and then heard Frank saying behind her, "Oh, you don't want to get her started on having all the chickens in the nest." He gave Mary a kiss on the cheek. "Mary is the ultimate sappy mom and wife too." Frank winked. "And I'm not too far behind with my fondness for a full house. We miss Elizabeth being around home. She has a contagiously energetic personality, which helps keep us from getting too lazy when she's around."

Mary politely interrupted, "And that girl has a gift of getting a party started! Damn, I miss her!"

Sarah chimed in, "Well as an outsider, it appears you two have done an amazing job raising your kids! The little bit I chatted with Billy this morning, he seems very polite and easy to talk to. I look forward to meeting Scotty and Frankie when they wake up from their post-hunting nap."

Even as a stranger, Sarah felt the depth of love between Mary and Frank as well as for their children. It made her miss her own family and look forward to the holidays when they would all be together again.

Not much time passed after Sarah's conversation with Frank and Mary before their sons worked their way to the kitchen one at a time. After an hour of them waking up and chatting, more wine bottles were opened. The atmosphere was revitalizing, and the volume grew much louder while the guys, talking over each other, told stories of their abbreviated hunting trip. Just as there was a momentary lull in the conversations, the timer beeped. Sarah slipped the puffy grey oven mitts on each hand and grabbed the extra-large dish from the oven.

"You look like a pro, Sarah!" Billy complimented from the other side of the kitchen island.

Sarah laughed at Billy's comment. "Well, I hope the food tastes as good as it smells. I followed my mom's recipe. Actually, it was my grandma's recipe first, which is meant for a large family. I assume the appetites of four men would be equivalent to a large family." Sarah smirked, nodding across the oversized island at the handsome faces staring back at her. Her eyes held a bit longer on Billy. *Damn, he's cute!* she thought.

Mary stood next to Sarah and leaned against the island. She showered the chef with compliments on her organization skills and attention to detail in the kitchen.

"Aw, thanks, Mary! That's sweet of you to say." She paused briefly and then lifted both hands in excitement. "Let's dive in! Frank, would you like to fill your plate first?" Sarah handed a plate to Frank.

"Though I'm honored you asked, I'm old fashion and believe the ladies should go first. Plus, it teaches my boys a little patience, even with hungry bellies." Frank stepped back and gestured for Mary and Sarah to go before him. "You two beautiful ladies can start."

Sarah blushed a bit and graciously accepted the offer.

The night went on as effortlessly as the whole day. They stayed at the table long after dinner was done just chatting and drinking wine. "Well, so much for driving back to Chicago tonight. It's way more fun here. And at this point, I'm thinking I shouldn't be driving anyway," Billy said with a smile.

Mary, sitting next to Billy, leaned over and gave him a one-arm hug. "Having you around for the night sounds just perfect to me. And on that note, more wine?" She poured what was left of the bottle into Billy's glass.

Frankie, Scotty, and Billy cleared the dinner plates and came back with a tiramisu dessert that Sarah also made. "Sarah, that dinner was so good, but this dessert looks even better!" Frankie said with his soft-spoken tone.

"Thanks, Frankie. Enjoy it!" she replied. The rest joined Frankie in offering their compliments to the chef.

Mary joked with Sarah about still wearing her apron through dinner. "Sarah, you look like you're ready to start cooking again with your apron still on. After a meal like this, I'd love to hire you as our personal chef."

Sarah replied, "It's the least I can do for you taking me in after the rental house fiasco. And, as for the apron, I have a funny story about that." Sarah, a little wine drunk at this point, laughed out loud thinking about the apron wearing of her youth. "Growing up in a large family, aprons were just part of our dinner attire. 'Better to have a dirty apron than dirty clothes,' my mom always said." Sarah paused briefly. "In fact, if we showed up at the dinner table without an apron on, my dad would fine us a quarter. Of course, all proceeds would go to mass collections so we didn't feel too bad if we had to give up some of our own money. I seldom wear aprons anymore, but when I do, it's instilled in me to keep it on until after the meal."

Sarah laughed, and Mary interjected, "No way! That is very ironic because we had the same rule with my family growing up. Even as little kids, we wore tiny aprons and were fined if we forgot. Although our fine was a nickel. I guess inflation is a real thing." The whole group laughed at the similar stories. Mary continued, "I wish I would've kept those little aprons, but thankfully, I kept the one you're wearing now. That was one of my mom's. I have vivid memories of her wearing it, especially on holidays."

Sarah added, "I am honored that you let me wear this one. I'm pretty sure this apron has some magic in it because I don't think I've ever made a better dinner or dessert than I did tonight. Usually something is missing."

The group complimented Sarah once again and then all got up to stretch and eventually move their way to the sunroom after cleanup was done.

"Anyone in for a game of Euchre?" Billy asked and then looked at Sarah. "Sarah, do you know how to play Euchre?"

Sarah, hanging the apron back up, said, "My family used to play Sheepshead, and I heard it's similar to that. How about I watch you all play and see if I can catch on?" Billy invited Sarah to sit by him so he could teach her.

The game went on for an hour before the front door opened and in walked a pretty girl wearing medical scrubs. Scotty went to greet her and planted a sweet kiss on her cheek. The two came into the sunroom, and everyone greeted the girl warmly.

Mary even got off her chair to give her a hug. Then with her arm around the girl's shoulder, she directed her focus to Sarah. "Sarah, I'd like you to meet Scotty's girlfriend, Lacey. Lacey, this is Sarah. She's a new friend and guest." The girls made their introductions, and Mary continued, "Scotty put a plate in the warming drawer for you, Lacey. Sarah was our chef tonight!" Lacey offered her gratitude and said she was so hungry after her long shift at the hospital.

The rain made a pleasant sound on the rooftop, adding to the cozy feel of the night. Sarah caught on quickly to the game and became a valuable teammate. Before too long, Frankie excused himself, saying he unfortunately had to go to school in the morning.

"Your dad and I aren't too far behind you, Frankie," said Mary and then pointed to Scotty and Billy. "Are you guys exhausted, or did your naps tide you over?"

They both replied that they were good, and then Scotty asked Billy and Sarah if they wanted to play against him and Lacey. "Sarah, just so you know, we are the reigning champs around here."

They all laughed, and Sarah responded with a quick wit, "Sounds like a great challenge. I'm up for it. How about you, Billy?" She nodded at Billy.

They held each other's gaze before he smiled back and said, "Let's do this!" and started shuffling the cards.

"Enjoy the rest of the night, you four! Billy and Scotty, what time are you heading back tomorrow?" Mary asked while beginning her exit from the room.

"I am going to head out in the morning, but not too early, seeing as I am suppose to be on vacation anyway," Billy replied.

Scotty after him said, "Lacey is off the next two days so I think I'll stick around and sign into classes remotely as well."

Mary clapped her hands together and gleefully said, "Well on that note, I am going to bed a very happy and content mom! See you all in morning. Sleep well!" Mary offered hugs and good night wishes to all the kids and went off to bed.

Sarah, Billy, Scotty, and Lacey continued playing cards. The game was getting heated, now tied at nine to nine. "One more point to win the round!" Billy said. "Our deal!"

Billy dealt the cards and flipped a jack of diamonds for center card. Scotty, sitting to Billy's left, said, "Pass." Sarah showed a jack of hearts in her hand so confidently she demanded Billy to pick it up. The hand could be over quickly but they played it out. In the end Sarah and Billy won and took over as the champs.

The four sat at the table chatting for a while and laughing at shared stories. Sarah talked about how a friend of hers ran into a glass door, and though she felt bad for her, she couldn't help but laugh her ass off as she fetched her frozen peas to put on her upper lip. Sarah laughed at the memory of her friend bouncing off the door. "Please don't think I'm a bad person for laughing at other people's expense. I have a bizarre sense of humor sometimes."

Scotty and Lacey looked at each other and then pointed to Billy at the same time. Scotty said, "You sound just like Billy!"

Billy explained, "Oh my gosh, Sarah, if you find humor in those things, you have to watch this video!" He briefly stopped the game so she could watch a video of Frankie and his friend running into each other at a basketball game last year.

Sarah immediately laughed and then asked, "Obviously Frankie survived, but what about his friend?" She laughed again before continuing, "I'm telling you, people must think I'm horrible for laughing at the expense of others, but I seriously can't help it. Show me videos of people running into glass doors, and I will be laughing for hours. That is, of course, if I know they are okay." Sarah covered her face with both hands and shook her head from side to side while laughing again at the images of Frankie running into his friend.

"New game?" Scotty held up the deck and looked around the group.

"Yeah, we want to redeem ourselves after that close loss," Lacey piped up.

The group agreed to another round, and cards were dealt once again.

Sarah, cautious not to appear too nosy, politely directed conversations to Scotty and Lacey, "I apologize for my curious personality, but I'm a romantic at heart and enjoy hearing about people's love stories. Plus, it gives me great love connection material for future books. So, what's your love story?"

Scotty and Lacey looked at each other, trying to determine who would respond, when Scotty finally answered, "We've been dating about a year and a half, but have known each other since we were fifteen and sixteen. Initially, a mutual friend introduced us. Lacey's a year older and grew up thirty miles from here, so we didn't see each other too much. However, when we did, we had a total blast!"

Lacey blushed and then took over the conversation. "But one night, we unexpectedly ran into each other at Bear's Tavern, and the rest is history." Scotty gave Lacey a wink across the table.

"I'll toast to that!" Billy said lifting his glass. The glasses clinked.

"Okay, Sarah, now it's your turn. Any love interest in the life of our new friend and resident author?" Lacey asked with a timid sweetness. "Being a romantic at heart, you must have someone special who keeps the flame of love burning brightly."

Sarah responded, "Oh gosh, it's a long story. To keep it simple, I am not presently in a relationship. Honestly, the only romance going on in my life is between the two fictional characters in my book." Sarah laughed at herself. "I am writing about the imperfectly perfect life of two people who were brought together through their love of travel. It's a little sappy, but it's been fun to watch how the love connection of these two people just naturally unfolded. Very serendipitous!"

"I can't wait to read your book, Sarah!" Lacey said with enthusiasm. "You are beautiful and talented. What man wouldn't want to date you?" Lacey complimented.

Sarah blushed and redirected the attention from herself. "Thank you, Lacey! And you as well! Scotty's a lucky man."

Sarah nodded toward Scotty and he exclaimed, "Yes, I am!" while giving Lacey a flirty smile at the same time Billy gave Sarah a sweet smirk of his own.

"That covers three of the four of us. Billy, how about you? Is there a special someone in your life?" Sarah continued to facilitate the conversation.

"Oh, Sarah, there's too many to list. You must've missed the line of ladies waiting for me at the front door." Billy laughed.

Sarah gave him a sideways grin and replied, "That's funny, I actually thought those girls were here to see Frankie. I told them all to leave because he's dating me." They laughed at Sarah's comment and sipped more wine.

Billy quickly replied, "Frankie certainly has a way with the high school girls, but I'm pretty sure he wouldn't be able to land a woman such as you."

Sarah interjected and pointed to herself, "And by me, do you mean an old woman?" They all laughed.

Billy smiled at Sarah and explained, "Well, yes, of course I meant old. Old but beautiful!"

Sarah put her hand on her stomach as if to cover up the flutters from being seen.

When it was finally time to call it a night, Sarah went upstairs with a content feeling in her heart. She grinned as she thought back to the sweet comment Billy made and realized she hasn't felt a flutter like that in years. She was amazed she didn't get antsy during the evening with the nagging deadline hanging over her head. She didn't worry about it once and was happily surprised at how easy it was for her to just enjoy the moment.

Damn, what a great day! she thought as she crawled into bed. *I didn't have a worry all day!*

Sarah's thoughts were interrupted by what she believed was a light knock on the bedroom door. With the noise of the background fan, she wasn't sure so she sat still to see if there would be a second knock. There was! Sarah hopped out of bed, shuffling quietly to the door. She opened it without a thought yet was still surprised to see those captivating, soft eyes of Billy's looking back at her. "Oh, Billy!" She hesitated. "Everything okay?"

"Oh, I'm sorry, Sarah. I didn't mean to surprise you. I just wanted to tell you how much fun it was to have you around tonight. My mom said she really enjoys your company, and now I can see why," Billy said.

Sarah, wearing no makeup and having donned her oversized Boston University T-shirt, smiled and replied, "I was just thinking of what a great day it was around here. You guys certainly made the best of your early return from the hunting trip."

Billy backed up slightly, not to invade Sarah's personal space too much. "I may not see you in the morning before I head back to Chicago, but I wanted to wish you luck on finishing your book. And tell you I enjoyed meeting you."

Billy looked down at the floor and then back up at Sarah with an adorable expression that made her heart jump. *What is that about?* she wondered as she put her hand lightly on her belly once again as if to stop the flutter from happening. "It was nice to meet you too, Billy! Thanks for the fun laughs tonight, oh, and also for taking the risk of having me as your Euchre partner."

"It was my pleasure!" Billy smirked as he walked backward, holding her glance for a few moments. "Good night, Sarah," he said before turning toward his room.

Sarah slowly closed the door and leaned against it with a strange new feeling in her chest. *Holy shit. Am I crushing on this guy?* She walked back to bed smiling like a school girl who was just kissed for the first time. She basked in that moment for a few seconds when she heard the faint buzz of her phone. *Oh my gosh I haven't checked my phone all night.* She was relieved to see she only had one message. It was from Henry.

CHAPTER 15

Her mind racing, all Sarah could do was think about the events of the prior evening as she hit the pavement of the now-familiar path. She smiled at the thought of how much fun she had and how easy it was to be with Mary and her family. She reflected on how her desire to be an author had overwhelmed her in many ways, yet that perseverance was also the reason she ended up on this whirlwind of a writer's retreat.

Sarah's head pounded a bit with every step, so she decided to slow the pace and walk instead. She looked up to the sky to let the sun hit her face while she thought of all the places her love of writing had brought her. She had traveled the globe in her few years at the magazine, and places like Italy, England, Greece, and the Caribbean were highlighted so descriptively in her book as if she could feel herself walking in those places once again.

Sarah thought back to her many career searches early in college. She was convinced her path would go one of two directions—event planning or counseling, based on her years of planning social activities for friends as well as being their sounding board. Through either of those careers, she was convinced she'd discover her purpose for life.

Now as she looked back on all her years as a writer, Sarah realized she never thought her words could be her purpose.

She felt an independent satisfaction from every article she'd ever written. However, fulfilling a purpose would mean she should be doing it more for others rather than herself. *Is it possible for purpose to be found in the process of enjoyment?* As she looked through the trees, she thought back to a conversation she had with a career counselor in the spring of her freshmen year of college.

* * *

Frustrated with herself, she took her fifth type of personality test in a week, searching for the answer to the looming question of what she wanted to be when she grew up.

"Why the hell do I have to know this answer so young? I don't even know what I want for dinner much less what I want to do with my life!" Sarah said to the patient woman trying to offer her direction.

"You're almost done with this test, and then we'll calculate the results. Maybe it'll point out something the other four tests did not," the woman reassured her.

"I certainly hope so because I'm at a loss and I need to register for major-specific courses," Sarah snapped back but then caught herself and apologized. "I'm so sorry. I know you are just trying to help. When I have doubts, I tend to go back to a comment my high school guidance counselor said when I was a junior. She told me that I wasn't cut out for college. Sometimes I worry she was right." Sarah expressed defeat.

"Well, if it makes you feel better, in looking at your grades from this year, I think the exact opposite of your high school guidance counselor," the patient woman said while paging through her folder. "I think you are more than cut out for college. Also, you are not alone in your frustration. More kids your age than not are stumped with the career choice."

"Thanks for your supportive words," Sarah said, now getting antsy while sitting on a squeaky yellow vinyl chair. "There, I am done with the test! Fingers crossed it has some glaring new career direction for me."

The two looked over the results. Sarah said with an exasperated tone, "Are you kidding me? Again with top suggestion of being a writer. Though I love writing, it's just a hobby. Writing is my creative outlet, my chance to escape from the world. I don't want people reading my words." Sarah sighed and shook her head. "No way would I *ever* want people reading my words! The thought of that would create major anxiety."

The woman calmed Sarah with an optimistic reframe, "Sarah, this is actually great news! The hard part will be convincing yourself that your passion for writing may actually be your guide to purpose as well. Once you relinquish your expectations of the career you think you should have and accept that the answer that is right in front of you, you can open your mind to the endless possibilities for your future."

Sarah took a few deep breaths to calm herself down before rolling her shoulders back. "Thank you for that! I needed to have this conversation today. You are the expert in career guidance, and I think it's time I listen to you. Can you direct me where to look next?"

* * *

"And there it is! Another rewarding experience gained from loosening my reins of control in life," Sarah said, picking up her pace.

"Hey, girl, are you talking to yourself?" Billy said coming up behind her.

"Holy shit, Billy! You scared the crap out of me!" Sarah said, taking out one of her AirPods. "I was zoning out, per usual during my runs." She laughed. "Nice surprise to see you this morning. I thought you were heading back to Chicago." They jogged at a slow pace while chatting about the previous night and the similar headaches this morning.

"The weather is finally nice, so I decided I'd rather work from here today than from my small apartment," Billy said.

"I don't blame you. It is like a dream being at your parents' house," Sarah replied.

"Compared to the small city apartments, yes, it's definitely a dream. Although our places, in the big cities, have their advantages too. Night life is pretty awesome!" Billy said.

Sarah nodded, "Good point!"

"Speaking of night life, did I hear you tell my mom you have a friend in town tonight? I'm sorry. It's really none of my business. You don't need to answer that question," Billy said apologetically.

Sarah reached out and tapped Billy's arm. "No worries at all! And yes, I have a friend in town who asked me to join him for dinner tonight. As of now, he's planning to pick me up at your house around 5:30 p.m. Will you still be around then? I'm happy to introduce you!"

Billy gave a thumbs up. "Sounds like a plan if I don't head back to Chicago after work today. What's your friend's name?"

"Henry," Sarah answered and then provided a little background of her relationship with Henry.

"It sounds like Henry has been part of your life for a long time. Was it hard for you when he got engaged?" Billy inquired.

Sarah stopped walking and looked at Billy. "Honestly, I was a little shocked with how early in their relationship they got engaged. They had really only dated a few months. I don't know Erin well, but from what I understand, she is a sweetheart and, like Henry, she wants a traditional marriage and family life. I'm happy for him and for them as a couple, yet strangely enough, the relationship between Henry and me has gotten a little muddy since their engagement."

Sarah took a deep breath and continued walking.

"Full disclosure, I don't think I help the muddiness either. We're friends, and for the most part that's been a good thing, yet recently he's been making subtle remarks about us as a couple every time we chat or text. He used to make similar comments when we were in college, but he stopped for a year or two. The fact that he got engaged to Erin led me to believe he had put our relationship behind him. However, based on his recent comments, I am starting to think otherwise. See what I mean about it being muddy?"

They stopped walking again, and Billy turned to look directly into Sarah's eyes. "I do get it and appreciate you confiding in me. We don't know each other well, but what I have noticed in the little time since I met you is that you seem to have your life put together quite well. From an outsider's point of view, it sounds like maybe Henry knows this too and is making last-ditch efforts to draw you back to him before you are gone forever. I obviously don't know the guy, but it appears he's in desperation mode. Who knows? Maybe he's hoping he will catch you in a weak moment and you'll change your mind about getting back together with him."

Sarah released Billy's gaze and looked at her feet slightly kicking the road. She sighed and responded thoughtfully, "Billy, I've had similar concerns recently, but to hear you say it out loud reinforces my gut feeling. Thank you for your honesty and also for your compliments. As sad as it sounds, my intuition has been telling me that Henry has Erin as his backup plan. I'm thinking our conversation may have to be more direct tonight. Oh shoot! And speaking of Henry, I forgot to reply to his text last night. I guess I was just having too much fun and maybe a little too much wine as well," Sarah said as they walked up the driveway.

Standing at the front door, Sarah stopped and touched Billy's hand.

"Billy, thank you for the conversation. I apologize that I monopolized your running time with my chatter. I am usually more guarded, but you have a nonjudgmental way about you that makes it feel safe to open up. And I appreciate your perspective on my Henry situation as well."

Billy held eye contact. "I enjoyed talking with you. And no worries on cutting my run short. With my pounding head, I knew it wouldn't be one of my better outings."

When inside, Sarah looked back at Billy closing the door behind him. "I think this day might require an extra cup of coffee. Could I pour one for you as well?"

With their steaming mugs, Sarah and Billy walked upstairs. "Good luck with your writing today, Sarah! It should be a quiet day around here, so we can both get our stuff done."

Sarah concluded, "Here's to productive days!" They clinked their coffee mugs before walking to their separate bedrooms.

Before Sarah got distracted once again, she reached for her phone and began texting. *Good morning, Henry! Sorry for the delayed response. I look forward to seeing you tonight and catching up then. Safe travels to the Midwest today. Below is the address where I am staying...*

The day went by fast, and before Sarah knew it, she needed to get ready for dinner with Henry. She shut her computer down for the day and was content with the amount she was able to get done. Her focus was impeccable despite the slight hangover that lingered most of the day. *How am I going to handle the conversation tonight? Do I keep it light or use the opportunity to get right to the point?* Sarah pondered as the nerves in her stomach made themselves present. *It will be fine. I have to protect my boundaries and be strong.*

Sarah didn't anticipate going out during her writer's retreat week, so she had to accept she would be underdressed for the night. Henry usually dressed up, even in the most casual of occasions. "Here go's nothing! This is the best I can do," she said while looking at her reflection in the full-length mirror. She then turned off the bedroom light and headed downstairs to wait for Henry.

Sarah approached the kitchen full of Mary's family chatting freely about their days and helping Mary get dinner ready. They all greeted her and Mary, not seeing Sarah "done up" all week, complimented her, "Sarah, you look so gorgeous! That boy won't be able to keep his eyes off you over dinner."

Sarah thanked Mary while sharing a smirk with Billy. She knew they had the same thought about how things would go with Henry. "Shoot, I forgot my purse. I'll be right back." Sarah exclaimed. And while she was up there, she could hear Billy opening the front door and introducing himself to Henry.

"Come on in! Sarah just ran upstairs to grab something. She'll be right back down."

"Thanks, Billy. This is a cool house! I guess I didn't realize I'd be picking Sarah up at a big house filled with people. I thought she was at a little cottage by herself," Henry said with confusion.

Sarah heard him while she came down the stairs and apologized for not filling him in on the details. "It's a long story but I can fill you in over dinner. I see you met Billy. I'd like you to meet the rest of this wonderful family," Sarah said while walking Henry into the kitchen and confidently giving brief introductions as if she'd known them for years. "You all have a great evening. See you when I get back," Sarah called out as she and Henry left the house. She was almost to the car when she said, "Henry, please give me two seconds. I have to run back in for something." Sarah pushed on the front door to find Billy was shutting it behind them. She briefly stepped inside and said, "I forgot to ask if you are leaving tonight. If so, I wanted to say my goodbyes and thank you."

Billy replied, "You're welcome. Actually, I think I'm staying until Saturday morning. I forgot that Frankie has a play-off football game on Friday night."

"Okay, great!" Sarah said with enthusiasm. "Then I will see you after dinner. Wish me luck!" She smiled and walked back to the car.

CHAPTER 16

Sarah and Henry drove down the lake road slowly so Sarah could point out where the rental cottage was supposed to be. She explained how she first met Mary and summarized how the week had gone since Saturday. "I can't believe it's only Wednesday night. It feels like so much has happened this week," Sarah said with a beaming smile.

"You are glowing, Sarah! You seem to be having a great week!" Henry complimented. "Looks like your hobby-time away is paying off and bringing out your happy side."

Sarah graciously accepted his backhanded compliment and then found her mood instantly declined. Henry continued the conversation questioning why she was wearing leggings and a long sweater for dinner. "My intention was to stay in and write all week so I didn't need to pack nice clothes," she snapped at him.

"It's all good. My rep gave me a restaurant suggestion, but from the sounds of it there isn't anything high-end in this town, so I'll probably be overdressed," Henry said referring to his suit and tie.

Has he always been such a pompous ass? Sarah wondered. "I'm sure we will both be fine."

Henry's insecurities quickly subsided, and they were able to have a peaceful dinner catching up on life. Sarah cautiously shared the progress of her book, wondering if he would be condescending again. To her surprise, he was the exact opposite, supportive, and even asking questions. Sarah was relaxed in her chair, pleased with how the night had been going. "Thank you for asking me to join you tonight, Henry. It's been great to catch up!"

The waitress politely interrupted and asked if they would like to see the dessert menu.

They nodded and Sarah said, "Sure, thank you!" Sarah turned her attention back to Henry. "So, tell me, how are the wedding plans coming along? I'm sure Erin is getting very excited!"

She noticed a sudden change in Henry's mannerisms. He was almost jittery as he shifted in his chair and wouldn't look at her when he spoke. "Oh, she's getting excited!" he responded and quickly changed the subject.

Henry propped his elbows on the table with his chin rested on top of his hands to get closer to Sarah. "Sarah, I know our relationship has been confusing through the years, but I want you to know how much I value your friendship. I love Erin, but you have to know that I will always love you too. You and I have a history together, and I never want to lose the bond we created years back. Please tell me you'll stay in my life once I'm a married man," he pleaded.

"Henry, you were right when you said things were confusing, but we can put that behind us and be friends even when you're a married man." Sarah hesitated and then mimicked his posture, putting her elbows on the table. "However, I think you need to promise yourself and me that there will be no more comments about how it should be you and me together. That will just continue to add useless confusion to our friendship."

Henry nodded in agreement and then sat back in his chair, creating a distance between them.

Before he could respond, Sarah continued, "Henry, you know we want different things in life, and more importantly, Erin deserves to have a man who loves only her. She shouldn't ever have to worry about sharing your heart or mind with another woman." Sarah's eyes softened, yet she noticed Henry wouldn't look directly at her. "I'm sure you understand where I'm coming from."

Once again Sarah mimicked Henry's posture, pushing herself back from the table and sitting straight back in her chair. An awkward silence followed when the waitress brought their desserts. They said thank you and sat in silence over their cheesecakes.

Henry put down his fork, looked at her, and said, "I understand where you are coming from. Trust me. I try to keep you in the friend category, yet it gets complicated. I know you get upset when I make comments about you and me. I'm sorry that I spurt those out. It happens without thinking."

Sarah started to interrupt when Henry held up his hand.

"Please, let me finish before I forget what I wanted to say." Once again, he took a deep breath before he continued, "I know I can be a jackass at times with the way I put you down or make light of your career. I apologize for all the times I made you second-guess yourself or made you feel small with my words. You know me well enough to understand I don't mean those things. It seems those comments are just a reactive response to my own insecurities. You deserve better than that, Sarah. I know how hard you've worked, and I respect you for achieving your goals. I guess, in a way, I'm envious because you have gotten all you've wanted in life."

Sarah interrupted, "As have you, Henry! Look at all you have in your life. You played a sport you loved in college, you have a very successful career, and you found a beautiful woman to spend the rest of your life with. Sounds to me like you've also gotten everything you wanted in life so far."

Henry nodded and reached across the table to touch Sarah's hands. "But I don't have you, Sarah. You are the first one who shared my dreams, and like I said before, I do love Erin, but I will always love you."

With a heavy heart, Sarah felt a twinge of old feelings come to her. She paused to absorb Henry's words while tears slowly rolled down her cheeks.

Sarah wiped away her tears, took a deep breath to center herself, and responded, "Thank you for your thoughtful words, Henry. You know I will always love you, too, but it's not the same love I had years ago. For that reason, maintaining a friendship may be more challenging than either of us wants right now."

Henry let go of Sarah's hand to sign off on the check. "I know that, Sarah, but I still need you in my life. I can't make you love me the way you used to, and I'm still trying to accept that. I just needed to express how I was feeling just in case you had a change of heart while away alone at your little retreat. But based on the people at that house, you obviously haven't been alone at all. And that guy Billy… Was it your plan to meet up with him all along?"

Sarah felt the sensitivity in her heart be replaced with anger as she stood up from the table and pointed to Henry. "Comments like those are unnecessary and irritate the hell out of me. And the way you use the word 'little' is demeaning and leads me to believe you don't really respect me at all like you said." Winded from anger, she took a breath and concluded, "And Billy has been more of a gentleman in the thirty-six hours I've known him than you have been in years."

She walked off fast, through the restaurant, and out to the parking lot. Henry caught up with her at the car. "What did I say?"

Sarah stopped at the passenger door and turned to him. Her voice escalated. "You don't even realize what you said, Henry? That's sad. Your knee-jerk reaction to be a condescending ass has run its course with me!" She paused briefly and quieted her tone. "Thanks for dinner, but please take me back to Mary's now."

The silence was deafening while Henry drove the fifteen minutes to Mary's house. He pulled into the driveway and could see through the window that people were milling around in the house. "Sarah, I wish I could do better for you. I understand what you mean by my words, but I think you sometimes blow things out of proportion. You know I respect you and your choices."

Sarah looked down at her folded hands and then up at him. "You have a strange way of showing you respect me, Henry. Sorry that you think I blow things out of proportion. I can't change your perception." She stepped out of the car and said, "Thanks for dinner, Henry. Safe travels back to Boston." Without looking back, she walked into the house.

CHAPTER 17

Sarah entered a cheery house full of positive energy. She heard Mary laughing just as she saw her walking in the door. "Sarah, you're back!" She started laughing again while waving Sarah over to join in on the conversation. "I was just telling everyone about our yellow chair rescue efforts."

Mary finished her part of the story when Sarah interjected, "Did you mention the wind gust that almost blew us both sideways off the pier?" Sarah chuckled.

With the family gathered around the island cleaning up after their dinner, it felt like home to Sarah. She watched them all interact and help each other while she thought, *I just left a man who used to feel like family yet now feels more like a stranger. And these strangers here feel more like home, more like family.* Sarah shook her head slightly trying to rid her thoughts of Henry and just enjoy what was right in front of her.

"So how was your night, Sarah?" Mary asked.

Sarah simply responded, "It was fine. I'm happy to be back here, though. It looks like I got back just in time for some cards." She looked over Mary's shoulder to see that Billy had moved into the sunroom and was shuffling the deck.

Billy overheard Sarah and said, "Yep, just in time for the champs to dominate once again. Sarah, would you be my partner again? Our next victims will be Dad and Frankie."

Sarah smiled and responded, "Absolutely! I'll be right there." She quickly ran upstairs to change her clothes. She heard a muffled buzz from inside her purse. She knew it was her phone. *That'll have to wait,* she thought as she rushed to get back downstairs. "Let's do this, Billy!" Sarah said with excitement as she walked into the sunroom.

The rest of the night went along similarly to the night before with laughs and competitive jabs yet with less wine. Frankie, Frank, and Mary headed out for bed while the other four played another game of cards, which turned into conversations sitting around in the sunroom. Sarah was able to get to know Scotty and Lacey a little better, and the conversation moved to Elizabeth.

"As expected, she and I have that 'twin power' going, so her being gone this semester has been strange for me. The time zone change gets a little challenging when we want to chat, but we are making it work," Scotty said. "I miss her and her energetic spark so much."

Sarah spoke of her study abroad experience. "Though it's hard on all of you and most likely on Elizabeth, too, she will never regret taking this time for herself. My parents told me they immediately noticed I was a more confident and content person when I returned. Although I didn't discover the 'purpose' to life as I'd hoped being over there," Sarah said while making quote marks, "Italy did reinforce my true love of travel. During that time away I decided my career would definitely have to intertwine my two loves, writing and travel."

Billy adjusted his position on his mom's favorite chair. "Our mom and dad love to travel and have instilled that into us as well. They said their favorite place to visit thus far was St. John in the Virgin Islands. They wanted to take us shortly after their trip, but the hurricane in 2017 destroyed the little island. Maybe someday we will get to go."

Sarah's eyes opened wide. "It's funny you should say that about St. John, as it's one of my favorite places as well. I certainly hope you all get to visit there someday. My only suggestion is go for longer than two days." She smiled and then told them her story of the work trip that fell over Christmas Eve.

Lacey complimented Sarah on her accomplishments made in a few short years. "I bet it was a relief when you found a job that combined travel and writing."

"Thanks, Lacey!" Sarah smiled and pulled both legs underneath her on the couch. "It's been quite a rewarding career and a great time in my life to put on the miles."

Lacey smiled at Sarah and said, "I love being a nurse, but some days I wish I could travel more and see the world. It's just not in the cards right now."

After a brief moment of silence Billy exclaimed, "Well, speaking of cards, you all up for another game?"

Scotty yawned. "I think we are out, dude. Time to get some sleep." He stood up and grabbed Lacey's hand to help her up as well. "Plus, I'm not sure Lacey and I can handle another ego hit by losing one more game to you two." They all laughed while Lacey and Scotty walked out of the room. "Good night, you two!" Scotty waved back

"Good night!" Lacey exclaimed while following Scotty.

Sarah and Billy remained in the sunroom. Billy moved from the chair to the couch where Lacey had been sitting next to Sarah. "Euchre champs once again!" he said while offering her a high-five.

"You know it!" Sarah said, returning the hand slap. They both smiled and then sat quietly for a brief moment.

Billy took a deep breath and tried to remain nonchalantly leaned back while he crossed one leg over the other and rested his arm on the back of the couch. "So how was your time with Henry? Everyone play nice?"

They both laughed and Sarah replied, "I appreciate you asking. I think I just need to let things simmer a bit. Honestly, I'm frustrated as heck with him. It's odd because we have so much history between us, yet at times, I feel I hardly know him." Sarah filled Billy in on the details of the conversations with Henry. "I guess maybe I do blow things out of proportion. I let his words get under my skin. For a guy I'm choosing to walk away from, I certainly put a lot of merit in his opinions of me."

Billy lifted his leg onto the couch as he turned more in Sarah's direction. "Sarah, you seem like a very intelligent woman with a good head on your shoulders. Maybe it's time you be brutally honest with yourself and make a decision where you want Henry to be in your life. For some reason you still allow yourself to be tethered to this guy, and it noticeably brings you stress. Once you give yourself time to think it all the way through, it may become clear how you want to proceed with your relationship." Billy gave Sarah a sympathetic side smile.

Sarah looked into Billy's understanding blue eyes and gently tapped the arm still resting on the couch. "Thank you so much for your perspective, Billy. You seem to get it! And your advice is spot on. I do need to take the time to think it all the way through. I just push the thoughts of Henry away because they no longer bring me joy. Maybe I just tolerate him because of our history, which is no reason to hold onto any relationship."

Sarah smiled at Billy and continued while they both started toward the kitchen.

"You are quite a guy, Billy Thomas! Why in the world don't you have a special someone in your life?"

Billy shut off the kitchen lights as they walked toward the steps. He stopped and looked at Sarah with a straight expression. "I guess I'm waiting for it to feel right. I'm done wasting time on surface relationships. I'm ready for something with more depth." He gave his familiar sideways smirk and started upstairs.

Sarah followed and quietly said good night before walking to Elizabeth's room.

"Goodnight, Sarah. I hope you sleep well. Maybe tomorrow you'll have more clarity about the Henry situation."

Sarah leaned against the doorframe momentarily. "Thank you for being my sounding board today. I appreciate your objective viewpoint." She backed into the bedroom but before closing the door said, "Sleep well."

When in Elizabeth's bedroom, Sarah grabbed her phone and saw a few texts from friends as well as her mom and Henry. Still irritated with Henry, she was going to wait to read his messages, but her curiosity prevailed. She clicked on his first text.

Henry: *I AM SORRY, SARAH!*

Henry: *Please check your email.*

Sarah closed out of her text window and opened her email. It didn't have a subject, just a long message:

Sarah, I am so sorry for my flippant use of words that probably came across as passive-aggressive. I wish I didn't have that major character flaw, but I do. In some way, I have always had that tendency when frustrated or at a loss of control. I thought we had a great night. I just wish it would've ended better.

I was not truly honest with you about the timing of my work meeting. I scheduled it a few days ago once I saw your location for the week. I did meet with a rep, but that wasn't the purpose of my visit. I had expectations in mind when traveling to see you, yet none of those were achieved. I should know better than to have expectations of you, as you have inadvertently shown me over the past five or so years that your heart and mind are at a different place than mine. I was just hoping that being together in a place away from familiarity of home would strike up a spark again. Even though you have told me, plenty of times, that you don't feel the same as you used to, I needed to know that I tried my hardest to prove how much you mean to me.

Obviously, we didn't get married right out of college like we originally planned in our earlier years. Now that we are twenty-seven, and still not married, I thought maybe you would be content with the years you worked and ready to settle into the life we dreamt about. I thought maybe you found the purpose you've been searching for since I met you and would be ready to step into a new chapter, finding a new purpose.

Sarah, tonight when you talked about writing your book as well as your recent travels, I saw a happiness in your eyes that told me you weren't ready to give it up any time soon. At that moment in our conversation, I felt my defenses go up and, without much thought, offered spiteful words. Though my heart is heavy, I believe I have the answers I need to finally move on once and for all. But before I move forward, I need to know that you, my first love, will not, in turn, be my last love as well.

Sarah reread the message from Henry one more time and then put her phone down. At this point she was too emotionally exhausted to text anybody other than her mom.

She asked if she could call her tomorrow and then crawled under the covers while a few tears dropped from her eyes. She knew in her heart what she wanted. Therefore, she would not hesitate to reply to Henry with a clear mind in the morning.

CHAPTER 18

Sarah rolled her eyes as she watched the rain drops bounce off the lake, mirroring her own feelings. The chilly morning found her exasperated. She'd tossed and turned all night, struggling to push away the thoughts of Henry's email.

Maybe Henry was right. Maybe she did blow things out of proportion? Perhaps it was easier to walk away by portraying him as an unsupportive jerk. But then again, maybe that's all he really was.

Sarah opened the email and read Henry's words one more time. She started clicking away a response, thinking of what it would feel like to see Henry marrying Erin. She'd seen them together in social settings, and it had not bothered her at all, but a wedding would be different. She knew that.

As Sarah stumbled for the right words to type, she remembered she owed her mom a call this morning. *She can give me some insight on how to respond to Henry. I'll call her in a few minutes.* "But first I need coffee!"

Sarah pushed the computer to the back of the desk and jotted down some thoughts on a legal pad before they slipped her mind. Then she dropped her pen and went in search of her mug full of happiness.

Though the outside was dreary, the kitchen had a bright and cheery atmosphere with the lights on and country music playing low on the ceiling speakers. "Looks like another one of those perfect writing days, Mary," Sarah said approaching the island.

"Good morning, Sarah!" Mary said with a newspaper sprawled out in front of her. "I couldn't agree more about being a perfect writing day. It is supposed to rain like this most of today and should be quiet around the house. Billy was just down here and said he has a couple of last-minute phone meetings today, so he will be working in his room most of the day. And I think Scotty and Lacey talked about shopping."

Mary rolled her eyes and folded up the newspaper.

"I think I've read enough. The news is more depressing than the weather these days." She quickly redirected her attention to Sarah. "On a positive note, how's the editing going? I know you weren't counting on being in the midst of a house full of activity, so I hope you aren't too far behind."

Sarah patted Mary's arm that was resting on the island. "Not to worry, Mary. It will all get done in the next two days, just in time for 'submit Saturday.' My flight heads out of Chicago late Saturday afternoon, and I plan to send the manuscript over to the publisher before I leave. I hope to get a bulk of it done in the next twenty-four hours. This weather is a gift from God. No run today, so I will head to the keyboard shortly."

"Oh good! It sounds like you have a clear plan. Also, if time allows, we'd love to take you out for dinner tomorrow for your last night. Frankie has a football game, and you are welcome to join us for that as well after dinner," Mary offered.

"That sounds terrific! That will give me motivation to focus today," Sarah said before taking a sip of her coffee. "On that note, I will take the coffee upstairs and get to work.

Thanks for making it once again. I am going to miss this when I go back to Boston."

Sarah felt her shoulders tighten knowing she needed to address things with Henry before she could clearly focus on her book revisions. She didn't want to be dealing with this right now yet strongly believed there was divine reasoning for everything. *A chat with my mom will help.*

Listening to the phone ring in her ear, Sarah glanced down at her notes at the same time her mom answered. "Hi, Mom, how are things at home?"

Sarah's mom was very chatty this morning and updated her on things going on around home. She mentioned that she and Sarah's dad were planning their next adventure for the upcoming year with hopes to take a Mediterranean cruise if weather allowed. "If the cruise doesn't happen, we'll visit by plane and train instead. As you know, Sarah, we have this vacation bucket list just waiting for items to be checked off," Sarah's mom explained.

"Hmm, I wonder where I get my travel bug from, Mom?" Sarah jokingly interjected.

Her mom carried on the conversation. She also updated Sarah on every niece and nephew's sports activities. Sarah rolled her eyes as she grew impatient. *I am such a brat for being impatient,* she thought but then decided to tune in a little closer to the stories.

My turn, she thought as her mom said, "Sorry for rambling. How are you, dear? I miss you. I hope your time away has been as productive as you hoped it would be." Sarah filled her in on all that occurred since they last spoke a couple days ago. She told her about the guys coming home, her making dinner for the group, as well as learning to play Euchre. She mentioned how nice Mary's husband and sons had been to her as well as dinner with Henry.

Then Sarah paused to gather her thoughts and took a deep breath. "Actually, Mom, as much as I love talking about the fun stuff, I need to discuss something else with you."

After a brief moment of silence Sarah's mom asked, "Sure, honey, I'm here for you. Is everything all right?"

Sarah stared out the bedroom window at the yellow chairs on the lawn and continued to tell her mom about the dinner conversation with Henry, following up with the email. She normally wouldn't share such specifics, but she needed to give her mom context and quickly.

"In the email, Henry brought up logical points to explain where his head is at. Honestly, I have felt his grip tightening on our friendship lately and now understand why. That being said, it is no longer a healthy friendship. And for a man who has committed to marrying another woman, his expressions of love for me have been displaced. I understand where it is coming from, but I am losing respect in his commitment to Erin and in him as a person. If I'm being truly honest with myself, I haven't really respected Henry since he first downplayed my love of writing and my career in general."

Sarah was finding herself choked up.

"Mom, I know you and Dad have always thought that Henry would be a great fit for me, and long ago I believed that myself. It just isn't there for me anymore." Sarah paused to catch her breath. "Henry's email confirmed my intuition that he has been holding out hope I would change my mind and come back to him at the last minute. Maybe he's more romantic than I gave him credit for, but truthfully, what he wants is for me to fit into his plan." Sarah was crying now. "I'm sorry for being emotional. Does any of this make sense? "

Sarah's mom paused briefly and then sighed into the phone before replying. "Sarah, it's been a while since we spoke in depth about Henry, and I couldn't be more thankful for you sharing all of this with me now. I've been waiting for you to come to this point. You are such a sweetheart. I feel horrible you've thought, this whole time, we wanted you to end up with Henry. Yes, we have made comments through the years about the perfect love story, but that's because it's what we thought you wanted."

"I know that now, Mom, but…" Sarah began.

Sarah's mom politely interrupted, "Never, in a million years, would we have wanted you to settle for anyone for our sake, much less someone you didn't love or respect. I feel just horrible that you've held onto that belief all this time."

Sarah's emotions had subsided slightly so she could clearly respond. "Well, Mom, if I'm truly being honest with myself, I think I was trying to create a love story similar to yours and dad's. The dream of marrying your high school sweetheart and living a magical life together seemed perfect when I was eighteen. However, it's not my reality right now."

Sarah's mom's tone softened. "First of all, you get to create your own love story, my dear. Our story belongs to us, and your story will belong to you someday as well."

Sarah sniffled. "Very true!"

Sarah's mom continued, "And also, as cliché as it sounds, everything happens for a reason. Maybe you needed to get to this point in your life to confidently give yourself permission to let him go, once and for all. I know it won't be easy, but I bet you'll feel better once you remove the weight of your relationship with Henry."

Sarah calmed down, taking deep breaths, as a smile tugged at her lips. "What would I do without you?" She stood up, looking out the window with new energy. Even the yellow chairs seem to be brighter. "You know what? You're right!"

Ping, the sound of Sarah's phone notified her of a text message. Since she was talking to her mom with her headphones on, she quickly saw the text come up on her screen.

"Wait, oh my gosh, Mom, you're not going to believe this!" Sarah exclaimed with a shocked voice. "I just got a text from a girl I went to college with, who, ironically is also friends with Henry's fiancée, Erin. She said Erin called off the wedding to Henry!"

"You're kidding!" Sarah's mom responded. "That must've just happened if he was talking about it with you last night."

"Well according to the text, she said Erin called off the wedding a week ago after finding out he's been cheating on her. Shit, Mom, that adds a whole new twist as to why he came to visit me. What an ass!" Sarah raised her voice.

"Good for Erin!" Sarah's mom said.

Sarah lifting her shoulders, her heart racing with anger. "That news will definitely change the content of my email reply. I am actually looking forward to sending it off today. And, once again, saved by divine timing. This will make walking away so much easier. Damn, what a jerk, trying to manipulate me into thinking he's giving our relationship one last attempt. He's desperate... and pathetic too! I think I'm gonna get this over with right now. Thanks for chatting with me Mom. I love you so much. I'll let you know how this all goes," Sarah concluded before opening up her laptop.

Sarah's response to Henry was short but impactful. She reviewed her words a few times and then, without hesitation, hit send. She took a deep breath and said, "It's out of my hands now. Let go, let God!"

Sarah knew with every ounce of her that she had done the right thing. The timing couldn't be more perfect to start a new chapter in her life.

CHAPTER 19

After putting her thoughts of Henry behind her, Sarah went on to have the most productive writing day since staying at Mary's. Her thoughts were clear, and the words flowed smoothly through her fingertips. She didn't even realize what time it was until she heard a knock on the bedroom door at 4:00 p.m. "Come in," she said with a raised tone.

In walked Billy with a plate full of snacks and a big glass of water. "I assumed you'd be starving and parched after being locked in this room all day."

Sarah replied, "That is so thoughtful of you. I got lost in my writing, I didn't even realize how late it had gotten. How was work for you today?"

Billy put the plate on the desk next to Sarah and sat on the window seat. "It was good. Just more than I thought I'd have to do seeing as though I was supposed to be gone on vacation. Oh well, I'm done for the day and looking forward to meeting up with some buddies in a couple of hours for pizza and beer."

"That sounds like a perfect way to spend your Thursday night!" Sarah asserted.

"It's always a good time seeing those guys." He paused briefly and continued, "I know you're slammed with a looming deadline, but if you want a little break, you're welcome to join us. The guys would be honored to be in the presence of a pretty woman such as you."

Sarah smiled as her face started to blush. "You know what, Billy? That sounds awesome! I'd love to meet your friends and see one of your local hangouts. Count me in!"

"Great! I won't bother you anymore so you can get more writing done." Billy stood up from the window seat and walked toward the door. Before leaving the room, he looked back at Sarah, "Let's plan to leave in a couple of hours." He quietly shut the door behind him.

Sarah stood up to stretch her legs. *What a nice guy!* Sarah thought while gazing at the still lake. She noticed the sun starting to reflect on the houses across the lake. Being so focused throughout the day, she didn't realize the rain had stopped. She pondered a few moments longer before diving back into her writing.

Sarah placed her hands on the keyboard. Still lost in thought, she flashed through the past week in her mind. She wondered how it would feel to leave Saturday. Would she and Mary stay connected? Would they actually pursue the idea of co-authoring a book? Since the boys arrived home, she and Mary hadn't had much time alone to chat. Sarah made a mental note to ask if she would have time tomorrow to catch up and then continued working for another hour.

Due to limited clothing options, Sarah just tossed on jeans with her Boston Red Sox ballcap and a sweatshirt that Mary had given her with the name of the lake on it. She looked in Elizabeth's mirror and was content with her choice of attire. She walked out of the room at the same time Billy was walking out of his. They caught eyes, and Sarah was relieved to see his outfit was similar to hers.

"Whew, I'm relieved I wasn't too underdressed. My clothing options are limited," Sarah said.

"You look perfect! Like you are ready for a night of beer and pizza with the guys," Billy offered. They walked downstairs together. "If you're ready, we can head out any time."

Mary was on her way to the kitchen when she bumped into Billy and Sarah coming downstairs. "You two look like you're ready for a fun night! Sarah, love the sweatshirt." Mary winked at her.

Sarah laughed and said, "Before we head out, I was wondering if you'd be around tomorrow during the day? It's been a busy few days, and I'd love to catch up before I leave on Saturday." The ladies made a plan for breakfast the next day, and then Billy gave Mary a big hug before they walked out the door.

It didn't take long before Sarah was getting picked on by Billy's friends. "I feel like one of the guys! They are so funny!" Sarah said when his friends walked away to grab some more drinks.

"Yeah, they're all right!" Billy smirked. "We make it a point to stay in contact as often as we can. Hopefully they can come to Chicago soon. The drinks are much more expensive, but it's good for them to let loose in the windy city once in a while." Billy pointed at his friends as they returned from the bar, "Sarah, if you wouldn't mind, could you fill these clowns in on your job? I told them a little bit about how you and my mom met, but I guess I really don't know much about your day-to-day job."

Sarah took a long gulp of her cold beer and expounded on how she was a writer for a travel magazine. She explained she was on vacation this week but next week would head out on a tour of the five top-rated spas in the United States. She figured it would be a perfectly timed trip after submitting her manuscript this weekend.

Billy's friends were so nice and genuinely interested in Sarah's job as well as the premise of her book. They asked questions about best and worst locations she's been to and even made some suggestions.

"So, Sarah, are you a baseball fan? What about doing a tour of the best Major League Baseball stadiums?" Billy's friend Teddy asked.

Sarah, feeling a little buzzed and sassy, replied, "Well, Teddy, I don't think I need to tour to find the best baseball stadium. I already know which one is the best…" She pointed to her cap. "Fenway Park, of course."

The group laughed and continued conversations for another hour. "Think it's time to call it a night," Teddy said as he tossed cash on the bar and picked up his sweatshirt from the chair.

"We're heading out as well," Billy responded. "As always, it's been fun! You all need to come to Chicago one of these weekends," Billy offered as he also tossed money on the bar.

On the way home, Billy took Sarah past his elementary and high school. He explained how he'd known most of the guys since preschool or kindergarten. Though most went to separate colleges, they managed to keep a solid friendship. Sarah shared how she had a similar set of friends. She still had a handful of great friends but didn't have much time for a social life with her travel schedule and book writing.

"Billy, I appreciate you asking me to join you tonight. I needed it more than I knew. It was a productive yet emotional day, so the laughs were a welcomed release," Sarah explained and then quickly changed subjects. "Hopefully it will be nice outside tomorrow. I'd like to get one last run in before leaving on Saturday."

Billy replied, "I agree on the run. I have another full day of work tomorrow, but starting it with a run would be perfect! And then mom told me you may join us for Frankie's game. Nothing like a good ole high school football game to finish off your week in the lovely Midwest!" They laughed as they walked into the quiet house.

Sarah and Billy talked for a few minutes more and agreed they needed to be productive in the morning, so it would be wise to hit the hay. At the top of the stairs Sarah lightly touched Billy's arm while quietly saying, "Thank you again for letting me tag along tonight." She paused briefly while their eyes connected. "I guess I'll see you in the morning. Sleep well."

Billy smirked and quietly said, "You too!" Billy watched Sarah walk to Elizabeth's room. She turned around, gave him a smile, and waved before shutting the door.

Once the door was shut, Sarah leaned against it and, with both hands on her head, questioned why she didn't make an attempt to kiss him earlier in the night. She had a few opportunities, yet something kept her from making the move.

Sarah walked toward the en suite bathroom and questioned if maybe she confused Billy's niceness for an interest in her. She shook her head and said, "Maybe it's for the better I didn't go for it, but damn, those eyes and these butterflies." She put her hand on her stomach. She thought she felt a connection between them. "This can't all be in my head."

Staring in the bathroom mirror, she took a breath to calm herself when she heard a knock on the bedroom door. "Oh my gosh, now what do I do?" she whispered and then walked slowly toward the door, wondering if it was a sign, a second chance. She slowly opened the door and frowned in confusion when nobody was there. *Oh my gosh, there wasn't a knock. I gotta get my head on straight,* she thought. As she started to close the door, her eye caught something on the floor.

It was a tube of her lip gloss and driver's license, and attached was a note. It was from Billy. *I thought you'd want these back. They were still in my pocket from earlier tonight when you asked me to hold onto them. - Billy*

CHAPTER 20

Sarah was lacing up her running shoes as she saw Frankie and Frank milling around the kitchen. "Wow, it's my lucky day waking early enough to catch you two before you head out for the day," Sarah joyfully said.

Frankie, tired like a normal teenage boy, grumbled something about her being a morning person and then laughed with her.

"I try to be a morning person, but it doesn't always happen that way," she said in reply. "Hey, Frankie, guess what? I'm going to your game tonight! I can't wait for the Friday night lights!"

"Wait! What? You are actually going to a high school football game during your vacation? Well, I'm honored. Maybe you will be a lucky charm. I haven't gotten a touchdown all season." Frankie, now waking up, had a lift in his tone.

"Good luck. Fingers crossed!" Sarah said, holding up her crossed fingers with both her hands. "Have a great day, gentlemen! I am off!" And she was out the door.

Sarah walked outside and breathed in the crisp fall morning air. She exhaled while looking up to the sky and started to walk for her warmup.

"What a strange dream!" Sarah said as snippets of her dream from last night flashed into her mind. She was at the same outdoor hotel bar in St. John where she'd watched the news about the Christmas Eve storm a couple years ago. She was sitting at the bar with that same blurry-faced man from her previous dream, and they were laughing while placing hypothetical bets on whatever game was showing on the TV. *That's right. We were betting on a Red Sox game.* She brushed it aside and began to jog.

Sarah had a spring in her step. Maybe it was the "vacation effect," or maybe it was just her finally making a decision to walk away from any relationship with Henry. *Or maybe it was Billy!* she thought with butterflies bouncing in her stomach.

She settled into a good stride and was back to Mary's in record time. She thought maybe she'd see Billy on her run again but no such luck. Probably better because she'd want to chat with him, yet she didn't have much time to get ready before her planned breakfast date with Mary.

The sun was shining brightly on their way to Mary's favorite coffee shop. "I'm looking forward to seeing this coffee shop from the inside today. It looked so cute from the outside last night. Billy and I drove around after hanging out with his buddies. He showed me some of his favorite places, but he also made it a point to show me one of yours as well," Sarah said while watching Mary's smile come across her face.

"That boy is something else! How sweet of him to think of me during your tour of the town." Mary turned the car into the parking lot. "Well, here it is!" She pointed to the building. As the women found their seats, Mary told Sarah about the excellent quiches and cappuccinos. "But, in my opinion, all the food and drinks are great here!"

"Sounds like I know what I'm ordering! Thanks for the suggestion," Sarah said, and with wide eyes she pointed at the glass case. "Oh maybe we could bring back some of these awesome-looking cinnamon rolls for the rest of the family too. It's all on me this morning!"

The two ladies rehashed their week for a while, and then Sarah finally mustered the courage to talk about what was really on her mind. "So, Mary, I know I'm not quite done with my first book, but I'm very excited at the thought of diving into a second one soon!" Sarah smiled while Mary smirked over her mug.

Mary finished her sip and then said, "I have been talking with Frank about this idea, and he thinks we should definitely pursue it! He agrees we have a unique story that could make a great novel or even a memoir, depending how personal we'd want to get."

Getting antsy in her seat, Sarah sat at the front of her chair and burst out, "Let's do it! I know we will make an amazing team!" Sarah noticed she might be a little too excited and settled back into her chair, taking a deep breath. "I think we should shake on it and worry about details and timeline some other day."

After some fun brainstorming and simple discussion, they finished up and headed home. When they walked in the house, Mary paused a moment and lightly reached for Sarah's arm. "I am very much looking forward to our future project and also dinner tonight, but before any of that, you have some work to do. Time to get yourself upstairs, young lady, and wrap up your labor of love," Mary said with a tone that reminded Sarah of her own mom.

They both laughed and Sarah replied, "Yes, ma'am!" and saluted Mary before trotting upstairs.

Sarah stopped in the hallway, noticing Billy's door was closed. For some reason, she felt a desire to see him. *Should I knock on the door?* She questioned herself as she searched her mind for an excuse but came up short. *He's probably in a meeting,* she convinced herself and then walked to Elizabeth's room.

The next five hours Sarah focused, undisturbed, on revisions until, at last, she typed her final words, "The end!"

"Holy shit! That's it! I am done!" Sarah exclaimed out loud to herself and then let out a louder, "Woohoo!"

Before Sarah realized there was someone knocking on her door, Mary and Billy entered in the midst of her doing a happy dance. She stopped abruptly, biting her lip when she noticed them. She looked back and forth between them and then focused in on Mary, "I did it! I finished!" Mary gave her a big hug, and they both did a happy dance together.

"You two are crazy! Fun, but crazy!" Billy said with a wide, proud smile. "Am I correct to say congratulations are in order?" Billy asked.

"Absolutely! I couldn't feel happier if I tried! I'm so thankful you two are here to share this moment with me!" Sarah touted with a beaming wide smile.

"We are honored to be part of it!" Mary exclaimed while hugging Sarah once again.

Billy offered Sarah a hug of congratulations before he left the room to tie up a few loose ends with work.

Mary stayed behind with Sarah. "It will be so fun to celebrate you at dinner!" she said.

Sarah sheepishly replied, "How about we celebrate us instead? Maybe we could break the news to your family about our future project!"

"Deal!" Mary gave Sarah a thumbs up and started walking toward Elizabeth's closet. "Sarah, I know you are limited on clothes, and from looking at you, I think you and Elizabeth are about the same size. She left some jeans and things here, so you are welcome to borrow something to wear tonight if you'd like."

Sarah, in awe of Mary's kindness, waited a moment and then said, "Mary, you are too sweet to me. I think I will take you up on the offer and try on a few of Elizabeth's things."

Shaking her head, Mary replied, "It's not a problem. Here are a few things that may work." She handed over an armful of jeans and tops.

Sarah stood outside the closet with the heaping clothes. "Thanks, Mary! Is there a certain attire I should consider for the restaurant?"

Mary started to exit the room but turned back. "We aren't too fancy around here, so anything that works for you will be great! We are heading to Frankie's game after dinner so we will, most likely, be wearing sweatshirts. And if you are still up for it, you're welcome to join us for the game."

Sarah said with confident delight, "I already told Frankie I'd be there. I'm looking forward to it! So maybe I should wear something football-ish." Sarah grinned before turning on her heels and heading toward Elizabeth's bed to drop the clothes.

Sarah looked in the mirror, holding up jeans and singing lyrics to a song she remembered her brothers and sisters jamming out to when they would get ready to go out with friends. She belted out the refrain when she heard Billy joining in from the doorway. He walked in carrying something and, without hesitation, joined in with Sarah. He stood by her in front of the full-length bedroom mirror as they leaned shoulder to shoulder, sharing one imaginary microphone that Billy symbolized using his thumb.

They turned to face each other and laughed at their performance. Within a moment, the room was silent except for the sound of exhilarated breathing from their duet. Their faces were close enough to feel each other's breath as their expressions turned stoic. The weight of their stare could only be held for a few moments, yet it spoke volumes.

They both looked down as Billy stepped back to put more distance between them. He shook his head as he took a deep breath, "Well, that was fun!" He smiled at her and held up the jersey in his hand. "Anyway, I heard you telling my mom you wanted to wear something football-ish. I have my old jersey from back in the day, when I played football. It's probably corny, but you are welcome to wear it."

Sarah realized she was holding her breath and chuckled at herself as she turned her attention to the item Billy was handing her. "Are you kidding? This is perfect! Thanks, Billy!" She grabbed the jersey from his hands. Then she hesitated briefly before asking, "Wait, will I have to fight off an ex-girlfriend from high school by wearing your jersey?"

Sarah smiled and Billy, blushing a bit, said, "Nope I think you should be just fine. No crazy ex-girlfriend to worry about."

Frankie was already with his team getting prepped for the game while the rest of his family, along with Lacey and Sarah, hopped in Frank's suburban headed for dinner. Along the way Sarah admired the scenery.

"From corn fields to golf courses and everything in between, you have it all within short distances around here. How sweet is that?" Sarah said to the group. "In Boston, I could be in my car for an hour and go only five miles."

Dinner was at a sports bar within walking distance from the football field. The walls were decorated with license plates from all over the United States as well as sports flags representing local and pro teams from around the state.

A table for six was waiting for them when they arrived. "I called ahead. Game days get crazy here," Mary explained.

After ordering drinks, Lacey and Sarah excused themselves to head to the restroom. When out of sight of the rest, Lacey lightly grabbed Sarah's arm and said, "I may be making this up, and truthfully it's none of my business, but I still have to ask, is there something brewing between you and Billy?"

Sarah smirked slightly trying to avoid blushing and replied, "What little I know of him, he seems like a great guy, and he's super cute. But to answer your question, no, there's nothing going on."

They walked into the restroom to wash their hands, talking along the way, when Lacey added, "Well, just for reference, I haven't seen Billy smile so much since I've known him, which has been about two years. Actually, Scotty was the one to point it out to me. He said he was surprised Billy stayed back home rather than going to Chicago. Apparently, he loves home but is somewhat of a workaholic, so he prefers to be working in the office when he can."

Sarah's eyes widened a bit and a smirk came easily across her face. "To be honest I'd think about it but not sure how Mary would take it. A stranger staying in her house and now hitting on her son." Lacey and Sarah laughed before approaching the table.

Sarah pulled out her chair and said quietly to Lacey sitting next to her, "Plus, I'm older than him."

Now seated, Lacey leaned over and whispered, "Age is just a number, and I'm pretty sure Mary wouldn't mind at all." And she offered Sarah a reassuring smile as they joined in with the conversation at the table.

Everyone had their drinks in hand when Mary raised hers saying, "I'd like to offer a toast to our new friend from New England. Sarah, God had a plan when he crossed our paths, and I am so very thankful for that. It's been a joy to have you staying with me and us this week. You are an absolute delight!"

Mary smiled with a teary grin before continuing, "It will be sad to see you go tomorrow, but we look forward to the release of your first novel. Here's to Sarah, our new friend *and* my co-author of our book, yet to be written!"

Everyone clinked their glasses followed by big swigs. It took a moment before the last bit of the toast registered with the crew. Then they started talking at the same time:

"Wait, what did you say?" Scotty questioned. "Did you say co-author?"

Billy, with excitement in his eyes, spoke over everyone while he looked between Sarah and Mary, "Are you two going to write a book together?"

Sarah nodded as Mary explained, "That's the plan! Sarah is going to help pull me out of author dormancy and, in exchange, I will offer legacy. We joked around that our book tour would be the best one yet!"

The family laughed and toasted once again, not only about the book idea but for the happiness they felt for Mary to get back into the industry.

Mary wrapped up her moment in the spotlight saying, "Just so you know, Dad and I did mention the co-authorship on the phone with Elizabeth last night and told Frankie this morning. They were both excited too." Mary nodded once again at Sarah, and a proud smile washed across her face.

Constant conversation accompanied the rest of dinner. It seemed to Sarah that time flew by, and before she even could offer a thank you, everyone was starting to get ready to leave for the game.

Sarah stood up before they did and in a polite manner said, "Please, everyone, before we head out, I just want to say something. I wanted to say thank you to each of you for making me feel so welcome in your home this week. I think we can all agree the situation was one of strange uniqueness." Sarah smiled and caught eyes with the whole group, pausing at Mary. "Yet Mary was so gracious and trusting to take me in. The rest of you offered me the same acceptance and warmth. I will never forget my week with all of you. *And, since I will be a writing partner with Mary, I assume this won't be our last time seeing one another.*"

"We are so excited for you both and can't wait to see what the future holds for your partnership," Frank said looking at Mary and Sarah. "Now, how about we go watch Frankie catch his first touchdown pass of the season!" Everyone cheered as they stood up from the table and continued their nonstop chatter while they walked to the football field.

CHAPTER 21

Billy pulled back nonchalantly from the group while they were entering the gates of the high school football field. He touched Sarah softly on the small of her back and asked if she had a quick second before they went in.

"Sure! I have all the time you'd like. Is everything okay?" she asked while waving the others to go ahead.

Billy pulled her gently away from the chaos of the entering crowd and said, "I just wanted to tell you how excited I am for you about the release of your first book. I obviously haven't known you long but see your passion for writing is evident. And quite admirable, I must say."

Billy gave a little smile, and Sarah immediately hugged him for his acknowledgment. He looked at her with intention.

"I also want to say thank you for encouraging my mom to come out of her writing cocoon. I was worried she would never get back into writing again, and like you, her love for it is visible." Billy paused briefly and continued, "Since we got home from the hunting trip, Mom has seemed less serious with life. She misses Elizabeth a ton, but I think you were a positive distraction for her. And now she has your new joint book project to think about too. So thank you!"

"Aw, your family seems like you all have so much love and respect amongst you. From what I've witnessed, you wear that love right on your sleeve, and your siblings seem to follow suit."

Sarah paused and, with a higher pitched, excited tone, said, "Actually, I should be thanking you for being so nice to me this week. Taking the chance of having me as your card partner, offering to let me join you for beer and pizza with the guys, and even giving me this awesome jersey to wear," Sarah said while tugging on the jersey she was wearing. "You seem like a pretty awesome guy, Billy Thomas, and I'm happy that chance allowed us to meet."

She smiled as she softened herself into Billy's arms for a hug. Billy held her a little longer than Sarah expected, but she didn't mind. He slightly released his embrace while looking down at her and gave her space to look up at him.

When Sarah looked back up at Billy, his expression had changed. He smiled with affection, yet he had a mesmerizing glimmer of hope in his eyes. "Sarah, I... I mean..." He took a moment to regroup while still holding her. He finally had the words ready, "Sarah, I–"

"Billy Boy!" He was interrupted by shouting in the distance. Billy rolled his eyes, visibly irritated by the distraction, and asked Sarah if they could briefly table their conversation for a moment.

"Hey, Billy, Sarah, wait for us!" It was Billy's friend Teddy. The two gradually released their embrace as Teddy and the others walked up to them. "Hmm, looks like we might've interrupted something. Sorry about that, kids." Teddy winked as they all laughed and walked into the game together.

That moment of distraction pulled them away from the time alone and into the flurry of activity surrounding the game. Sarah had a great time regardless but found herself preoccupied wondering what Billy was trying to say to her.

She didn't want to overthink the hug or the look in his eyes, so she went on. However, she was reminded of what Lacey mentioned to her earlier.

Sarah lost herself in the idea of the two of them, but then her mind flipped quickly to Henry. She hadn't heard from him after she sent the email. She imagined him reading it somewhere on his travels back to Boston. *Who knows, maybe it's exactly what he needed to move forward as well.* The cheerleaders interrupted her thoughts by firing up the fans.

Sarah could hear murmurs of conversations around her while her mind wandered back to the conversation with Henry at dinner. She tried to recall if they spoke much about his wedding. She couldn't remember many of the details, nor did she want to.

Within seconds, the Henry "thought bubble" was popped and replaced with the joyful image of Billy. With butterflies in her stomach, she looked at him seated next to her as he began cheering, "There he goes, oh my gosh, there he goes... he caught it! Holy shit, he got the touchdown pass! And with *one* hand! Holy shit, Sarah, did you see that?" They both joined in with the rest of the fans celebrating in the stands.

Mary gave Sarah a big hug full of excitement, and Frank leaned over and said, "Well, Sarah, I guess Frankie was right. You are a good luck charm!" and winked while high-fiving her and the friends around him.

Frankie's team won the playoff game. The family decided to continue with their celebration back at the sports bar and grill. Frankie and some teammates even joined them for postgame food.

Still beaming after his amazing touchdown catch, Frankie looked at Sarah and said, "Same time, same place next week,

Sarah? You are obviously my good luck charm!" He smiled, and she gave him a congratulatory hug.

"I'll see what I can do," Sarah replied, offering Frankie a wink before he went on to join his friends.

It was after midnight when the family finally got back home, still charged up about the win. "I don't even live in this town, and I'm still excited for the team, especially for Frankie. I can't imagine how the rest of you must feel," Sarah said while they were getting out of the truck in the garage. "What a terrific way to end my week here!"

As Sarah walked down the hall, she happily shouted ahead to Mary already in the kitchen, "Mary, I think we have more material for our story."

Mary yelled back at Sarah, "You got that right, girl. I think the book will practically write itself."

Everyone scattered to their respective rooms, saying their good nights. Sarah knew she had a little packing to do, but it wouldn't take long. She was going through the details of her return travel day, but the idea of leaving the beautiful home on the lake made her a little sad. However, she knew her new relationship with Mary offered hope she would be back.

Sarah's mind wandered to the earlier conversation with Billy. They had been so caught up in the game and celebration, they didn't have another moment alone. She didn't want to make a big deal out of it, but she was curious. *Should I go talk to him now? Would that be too forward, too presumptuous?*

"What the hell? I'm going for it." She gave herself a pep talk as she quietly opened Elizabeth's door and walked toward Billy's room.

With her hand resting on the doorknob, Sarah hesitated long enough to come to her senses. Though it wouldn't be a big deal to visit his room, she didn't want to cross a line of trust with her new friend and soon-to-be writing partner. Plus, Mary knew Sarah had been debating about Henry this week and didn't want to appear flippant with men, especially when one of them was her son.

CHAPTER 22

Sarah skimmed through her completed novel as a wave of confusing emotions bounced around in her, sadness and relief wrapped into one. She was extremely satisfied with her work yet dreaded the completion of her author's journey. She loved the whole process, even the tough moments where she wanted to toss in the towel.

Sarah paused for a brief moment, allowing the feeling of contentment to wash through her before she hit submit. She did it! From here on out, she would be on a fast track to printing and selling her first book. What a whirlwind it would be! She beamed with pride as she heard rumblings of chatter downstairs. Not wanting to linger any longer, she popped up from the desk chair and joined the others for her last morning at Mary's.

Sarah stopped quickly at the top of the steps, noticing Billy's bedroom door was open. Slightly embarrassed with herself that she felt the pull to visit his room last night, she thought, *That wouldn't have been a good thing.*

"Or would it?" she questioned softly to herself with a grin.

Almost frozen in motion, Sarah wondered if she should go see him in his room now or just head downstairs. She was still intrigued by what he was going to say to her before the football game, yet she didn't want to appear pathetic by asking him, so she continued down the stairs.

Besides Frankie, the rest of the family was around the island with their coffees and breakfast. "Sarah, good morning! Come join the rest of us," invited Mary. "Frank and I made a big breakfast for everyone before the mass exodus. It sounds like it will be back to Frank, Frankie, and me within a couple of hours." Mary made a brief pouty face.

Sarah walked over to Mary's side, offered her a one-arm hug of support, and rested her head on Mary's shoulder. Then she stood up straight, glancing at the faces around the island before picking up a plate. "Mary, Frank, the breakfast looks terrific!" Sarah filled up her plate and sat next to Billy, noticing the flutters in her stomach again.

Billy had both hands on his mug with an empty plate in front of him. He looked sweetly at Sarah. "Good morning. After the fun night out celebrating, I hope you weren't up too late reviewing your manuscript one last time."

Sarah smiled with a forkful of food in front of her and said, "It was a fun night, but once my head it the pillow, I was out!"

Billy's grin caused Sarah to wonder if maybe he knew she was outside his door last night.

Mary continued the conversation, briefly summarizing the past week. "Sarah, your head must be spinning with all that's occurred while you were staying here. It seems like a long time has passed since we met at the missing house. From the storms to the football game—it has been quite a blessing to have you around. God is in the details of life, and he most certainly had some fun with us this past week."

The group laughed before a few quiet moments of reflection settled on everyone. Sarah noticed a sadness in Mary's eyes and droopy shoulders from the group. The atmosphere shifted from lighthearted to melancholy, anticipating everyone's departures. She was familiar with that feeling when her own family disembarked from gatherings together. *Depressed yet also content,* she thought.

Scotty and Lacey were clearing their plates, and Billy put a plate of food into the warming drawer for Frankie when Mary blurted out, "Thank you so much for the help, kids, but I know you have busy days ahead. Please carry on. Dad and I will take care of clean-up." She gently shooed them from the kitchen.

Scotty and Lacey were going to head out soon, so they quickly schemed with Billy and Sarah to jump on Frankie's bed before leaving. Mary and Frank stood at the bottom of the stairs smiling, listening to the commotion above. Frankie pretended he was frustrated with the disturbance, yet they knew he loved every minute of it.

Billy brought his bags downstairs with a few minutes to spare before leaving. Sarah heard him tell his parents last night that he was meeting up with some work friends in Chicago that afternoon. Sarah would be about a half hour behind him heading the same direction. For a brief moment, she dreaded her travels back to Boston. *It's going to be a long week.* She stressed about stepping back into the real world while putting the rest of her things into her carry-on bag. She looked up to see Billy about to knock on the already open door.

"Hi again. I'm heading out and thought I'd say goodbye."

Sarah stood up while Billy walked toward her. She felt a nervousness in her stomach as he got closer. "It's been great getting to know you and your family, Billy. I don't think it has completely hit me just how blessed I am to have met your mom and all of you."

Billy looked at her with his captivating eyes and said, "Please know if you are ever in Chicago, you have an open invitation to stay at my place. I'd be happy to take you to some of my favorite beer and pizza bars." Their laughs were followed by an uncomfortable silence. "Best of luck with your book... I can't wait to read it!" He offered her a hug, and she reciprocated by hugging him tightly, as if to pause this moment for a while longer.

Now or never, Sarah thought as she slowly pulled away. "Last night before the game, you were starting to tell me something. Do you still want to talk about that?"

Billy took a step back so he could look into her eyes and then looked down at his feet. "It's nothing. I think I was caught up in the moment. It's all good."

Sarah's shoulders drooped slightly with disappointment, and she knew her expression showed it as well. "Are you sure? I don't have to leave for a half hour yet. I'd love to hear what you wanted to tell me."

He smiled at her and then said, "Naw, it's okay. It wasn't a big deal."

But Sarah wasn't convinced she believed it. She tried to match his flippant words by saying, "Okay. But if you change your mind and want to chat, we both have long drives ahead of us. You could always call me." She was trying to provoke him to talk.

Sarah wrote down her cell number on a Post-it note with a smiley face next to it and handed it to Billy. "I'm all packed up here, so I will just walk down with you."

They walked toward the bedroom door when Sarah stopped and turned around. She had to absorb her accommodations one more time. She sighed, smiled, and continued to walk with Billy.

Standing by the front door, Mary, Frank, Frankie, and Sarah all gave final hugs to Billy before watching him leave. Sarah glanced at Mary, seeing a tear of mixed emotions drift down her cheek. Mary looked at Sarah standing next to Frankie and said, after clearing her throat, "It doesn't matter how old my kids get. It's never easy to see them drive away from home." Mary hugged Frankie and joked, "I think I'm going to make you stay here forever."

Frankie hugged her in his sweet teenage way and said, "Mom, I'm sure you'll be ready for me to leave when the time comes." He winked.

Frank rolled his eyes yet smiled, saying, "Frankie, I'm pretty sure that will never happen."

Frank and Frankie went into the sunroom to watch college football while Sarah and Mary stayed by the front door reminiscing a bit more before Sarah left. Sarah told Mary what she said to Billy about all the goings-on of the week and the incredible blessings not completely hitting her yet.

"Watching you with your family gives me hope for my own future of becoming a mom. You, like my mom, don't hold back on your expressions of love toward your family. You are both strong women who taught me that it's okay to love with my whole heart without sacrificing a life of my own. If anything, you confirmed that, even in the midst of a stormy day, I still have lessons to be learned, love to be given, and laughs to be had." Sarah, with tears in her eyes now, laughed slightly at her last statement and said, "Hmm that was a good line. Maybe we should add that to the book." They laughed while wiping the tears from their cheeks.

Sarah went into the sunroom to give final hugs to Frank and Frankie before Mary walked her to her car. With the car door open, Sarah gave Mary a long embrace before saying,

"Who knows, Mary, once the details of the week settle in, I may understand what God's purpose is for my life. Hell, for all I know, I might meet the love of my life on my next business trip."

Mary looked at her with a confident little smirk and said, "Or, maybe you met him already." She winked at Sarah and offered her a wish of safe travels. "Please text me when you arrive safely in Boston. And, Sarah, thank you!" Mary shut the door, watching Sarah blow a kiss and wave before she drove off.

Sarah drove away from Mary's house and then stopped briefly where the missing house was supposed to be. She looked at the open lot filled with dirt and out at the beautiful little lake. After a moment, she smiled slightly and drove away.

Now on the interstate heading toward O'Hare, she thought about Billy. She thought about him driving on this same road just moments earlier. She thought about the first time they met and how familiar he seemed to her. She reflected briefly on what transpired with Henry and the needed finality to that relationship. Even though she didn't care what he was doing, she still wondered. She gave herself some grace, realizing this wonder was part of the process.

Sarah shook her head gently and smiled, as if to release those thoughts from her mind, when she was startled by her phone ringing. Sarah looked at her phone but didn't recognize the number, so she set it back down. Something pinged in her gut and she realized that area code was from Chicago. *Billy?* she wondered as she curiously answered it. "Hello."

"Sarah?" the voice on the phone said.

"Yes, it's Sarah."

The voice said, "Oh hi. This is the car rental company from Chicago returning your call from a couple of days ago." *Damn it!* Sarah thought. "Oh hi, thanks for calling me back. I actually was able to find an answer online." The voice nicely ended the call, and Sarah continued on driving, briefly let down with the thought it might've been Billy calling.

Sarah shifted around in her seat, feeling a bit ansty from the drive. She turned on the radio to distract herself and heard a song she remembered playing in Mary's tiny office the night she discovered that she was a famous author. *What a fricking week!* she thought.

Sarah even surprised herself with how easy it was to let go of her plans and adapt to her new surroundings and new friends. *Have I wasted my whole life controlling every detail, trying to chase a hypothetical purpose? Or did the chase lead me to Mary to find my purpose? Maybe my purpose was to meet Mary and write a book together?* Sarah continued to question herself and her choices. Her situation surrounding her writer's retreat was anything but planned or expected. She couldn't have written a story better than that. *Yet what's it all for?* she questioned again. *If I learned anything from my writer's retreat, it's that usually the best moments happen when I have no plan.*

Sarah sat up straight in her seat and at that moment was hit with a wave of clarity so powerful, it was like God answered all her questions at once. Sarah knew then and there she would live her life differently. It was time to loosen her proverbial grip on life. She made a mental commitment to herself that she would relinquish the expectations of how life should go and enjoy the opportunities that were right in front of her. "Let go, let God!" she said and then reiterated Mary's mantra out loud once again when her phone interrupted her.

Without looking at the number, she just answered it, "Hello."

"Sarah, is that you? It's Billy."

Sarah looked up to the sky and mouthed the words, *Thank you!* before she spoke into the phone. "Hi, Billy. How's your drive going?"

They had a surface conversation for a few moments, and then he said, "Well, you told me I should call if I changed my mind and wanted to chat. I actually had a thought and wanted to run it past you."

Sarah responded, "Oh now you have me intrigued. Whatcha thinking?"

"I know you have a busy week ahead and you're probably ready to get back to Boston, but…" He stopped talking.

"But?" Sarah encouraged him to continue.

"Shit, now that I hear myself talking, maybe it's not such a good idea," Billy offered as a bashful response.

Sarah quickly said, "How about you tell me what you're thinking, and I'll let you know if it's a good idea?"

Sarah could hear Billy sigh before he started talking, "Shit, I'm actually nervous all of a sudden. Okay, it's now or never." He paused briefly. "Knowing that you're on your way to O'Hare, I was wondering if you'd consider pushing your flight off another day and spend the night in downtown Chicago?"

"Hm, tempting," Sarah said followed by a long pause. "I love that idea, but think it's probably in my best interest to stick to my plan for the week. Could I get a raincheck?"

Billy responded saying, "Oh yeah, that's totally cool. I just thought I'd give it a shot since you were heading this direction anyway."

Sarah flashed back to the pep talk she just gave herself, about loosening her grip on plans and accepting opportunities. With an optimistic tone, she replied, "You know what, Billy? I do like that idea! How about you give me a few minutes to think about it? I am about five miles from the O'Hare turn off, so I don't have too long to work through the details, but I'll call you right back."

Sarah thought through her week ahead and the many things she wanted to do before leaving on her business trip. Her logical mind reminded her of the reasons why it would be irresponsible to stay, yet her gut gave her the opposing message. With the O'Hare exit less than a mile ahead, Sarah took a deep breath and flipped on her blinker. *Click, click, click* it sounded as she picked up her phone to call Billy.

Sarah heard his voice on the other end, "Hi, Sarah, so what did you decide?"

Still conflicted between logic and spontaneity, she responded.

ACKNOWLEDGMENTS

The Writer's Retreat was a labor of love only brought to fruition with the assistance of an all-star team of professors and editors from Creator Institute and New Degree Press. With sincere appreciation, I'd like to particularly thank Rebecca, Ilia, Colin, and Amanda for their patience and counseling efforts offered to me along this maiden voyage of book writing. Thank you for sharing your talents with me by way of suggestions, edits, and revisions, all made possible through Zoom and Quip.